Sholom Aleichem

TWAS 460

Sholom Aleichem

SHOLOM ALEICHEM

By JOSEPH BUTWIN
University of Washington
and
FRANCES BUTWIN

TWAYNE PUBLISHERS

A DIVISION OF G. K. HALL & CO., BOSTON

Library of Congress Cataloging in Publication Data

Butwin, Joseph, 1943–
  Sholom Aleichem.

  (Twayne's world authors series ; TWAS 460 : Yiddish
literature)
  Bibliography: p. 167–70.
  Includes index.
  1. Rabinowitz, Shalom, 1859–1916. 2. Authors,
Yiddish—Biography. II. Butwin, Frances, joint author.
II. Title.
PJ5129.R2Z565   839'.09'33 [B]   77–3495
ISBN 0–8057–6297–3

In Memory of Julius Butwin

Contents

About the Authors

Frances Butwin was born in Warsaw, Poland, in 1911 and came to the United States with her family in 1922. From Ellis Island the family went straight to Charleston, S.C. She received a B.A. from the College of Charleston in 1933. Upon her marriage that same year she moved to St. Paul, Minnesota, and has lived in Minnesota since then. In 1953 she received a B.S. in Library Science from the University of Minnesota and worked as a reference librarian in the Minneapolis Public Library for about twenty years.

Mrs. Butwin, with her husband, Julius Butwin, selected and translated a volume of stories by Sholom Aleichem which was published in 1946 under the title of *The Old Country*. Julius Butwin died in 1945 before this book came out. In 1949 Frances Butwin published another selection of Sholom Aleichem, *Tevye's Daughters,* and in 1952 a translation of Sholom Aleichem's novel, *Wandering Star.* In 1969 she published a book for young people, *The Jews in America.* She is now living in Minneapolis.

Joseph Butwin was born in 1943, attended the University of Minnesota and received his Ph.D. from Harvard University in 1970. He has published articles on English, French, and Yiddish literature. His work is primarily a study of comedy embodied in the figure of the clown. He teaches English literature at the University of Washington. Currently he is serving as a visiting professor at Vassar College.

Preface

How have I earned this honor that a world of people suddenly should become aware that on the other side of Boyberik not far from Anatevke there is a Jew named Tevye *der milkhiger?*
—*Katonti,* A Letter from Tevye to the author

Since Sholom Aleichem gave these words to his most well known character, that "world of people" has both diminished and expanded. The vast Yiddish-speaking population of eastern Europe has largely been destroyed by systematic murder and by emigration and absorption into other cultures. In another sense the world that knows Tevye has been multiplied since the 1940s by translations that bring him to an audience that does not read or speak Yiddish and is not necessarily Jewish. More recently, of course, a musical comedy performed on stage and on film has given the name of Tevye to the world of people who never read the Yiddish original or the translations.

Toward the end of the Second World War when it became evident that Tevye's world had been destroyed, it became equally evident that, if it were to be reconstructed at all, the task would be managed by writers. In 1943 Maurice Samuel recreated *The World of Sholom Aleichem* from the evidence of the stories and his own vast knowledge. Samuel's book stimulated translations by Julius and Frances Butwin. Shortly after the war Mark Zborowski and Elizabeth Herzog wrote an anthropological memorial to the *shtetl* based primarily on interviews with its survivors. Many studies of the life and letters of Hitler's victims have been written since, but none has the poignancy of those first contributions that grow out of the experience itself as creative answers to destruction.

Critics immediately after the war tended to make Sholom Aleichem's writing an anonymously constructed monument to the dead and to make of the author a legendary voice of the mute. "He was part of Russian Jewry," Samuel wrote. "He was Russian Jewry itself. It is hard to think of him as a 'writer.' He was the common people in utterance."[1] A decade later Irving Howe and

Eliezer Greenberg, who along with Maurice Samuel are the great disseminators of Yiddish culture in the English-speaking world, described Sholom Aleichem as "the great natural genius of Yiddish literature . . . one of the very few modern writers who could be said to speak for an entire people."[2] What these critics say about Sholom Aleichem is true. It is supported by the abundant testimony of earlier Yiddish critics. But to say that a writer is the representative voice of his people tells us very little about the literature that made him so. In fact it suggests an almost preliterary bard, a "great natural." The fact that Sholom Aleichem has continued to convince people that this is true is the result of a conscious effort on his part. How did Sholom Aleichem create the voice of the people? How has he convinced his readers that he is, to use his own term, the authentic *folks-shrayber,* "the people's writer"?

Sholom Aleichem's career as a writer began in the early 1880s when the word "pogrom" was coined to describe the thunderlike attacks on the Jews of western Russia. The outward violence of 1881 was followed by a new round of restrictive laws whose major effect was to depopulate the small towns of the Russian Pale and fill the cities as well as the emigrant ships. The terrible dislocation of Jewish life in those years shattered many people but it also provoked a great awakening of national, cultural, and political aspirations among Jews. If modern Yiddish literature came of age with the coming of age of this young writer, it is partly a coincidence of historical forces and partly the result of his own conscious effort to establish the almost nonexistent vernacular literature. The creation of a literature out of a language generally reserved for everyday speech required standards which he set as an editor of his own annual and imposed upon himself as a writer. A rigorous critic of the spurious and sentimental in the popular Yiddish fiction of his day, he nevertheless made his own appeal to the popular experience of Yiddish speakers.

The new Yiddish literature would often base itself in the life of the small town (*shtetl*) where Sholom Aleichem, like so many of his readers, had passed his youth. The *shtetl,* like youth, was already passing into the collective memory of his generation. From his early stories about childhood to the autobiography which he wrote shortly before he died Sholom Aleichem perpetuates that memory in his own experience. The experience of childhood described in the stories and in the autobiography includes the genesis of a writer who associates himself with people on the fringe of the community that he describes. His early mentors are orphans and outsiders who speak to his own impulse to release himself from the constraints placed on him by the respectability of his family and by his required education. Thanks to his own father's fall from financial grace and the death of his mother he had himself known the condition of orphanage and displacement that places a young Jew outside the charmed circle of social prestige and at the same time puts him directly in the mainstream of a people that had come to think of itself as communally displaced, communally orphaned.

This, after all, is life in the diaspora, a continuous condition shared by all Russian Jews, the great majority of whom were paupers. The Jewish pauper, kept at a distance from the "indigenous" population of Russians and kept on the edge of a Jewish community that values wealth and learning, leads a life both at the center and on the periphery of his culture. Sholom Aleichem created his comedy around the condition of poverty which he knew to be deplorable. We laugh insofar as we are made to recognize the continual expectation of Messianic deliverance sustained by these paupers in the midst of utter squalor. Messianic expectations may be reinforced by the acceleration of unhappy accidents which in the life of the clown are also funny. This is not to say that Sholom Aleichem mocks poverty. Laughter stops when it becomes clear that instant deliverance is unlikely and that life is only squalid.

The social orientation of Sholom Aleichem's paupers is really quite like that of his artists if we understand that the artist in this world is not a sublime specialist. The artist in Sholom Aleichem is everyman. He is not so much an author as a storyteller whose voice is easily recognized as that of a man or a woman talking. Many of the stories come to us as if they were monologues written down by the writer but originally spoken by a poultrywoman, a traveling salesman, or a dairyman. It is through a consciously created style known to Russian critics as *skaz* ("speech") that Sholom Aleichem creates the impression that he is not "a 'writer' [but] the common people in utterance."

The Yiddish *folks-shrayber* is a creature of the modern world. He recreates the folk voice with the self-consciousness and the distance acknowledged by those of his contemporaries who went out in the small towns of the Ukraine carrying with them new recording devices for the purpose of capturing the voice of the people before it was lost. A photograph in the YIVO archives shows two young men sitting before a log cabin with a group of children. The great horn of an early gramophone recorder is aimed at the children. The presence of this machine and the implied presence of the photographer suggest the distance and the proximity of the Yiddish artist who both records and creates from a modern perspective. As readers we are allowed both intimate exposure and ironic distance from the folk. If we limit ourselves to a description of Sholom Aleichem as the popular voice captured in print we are following cues that he himself deliberately left, but we are not prepared to understand the conscious acts of the artist which it is the purpose of this book to describe.

Chronology

1859   Sholom Rabinovitsh born in Pereyaslav, *gubernia* of Poltava, March 2.

1877   Employed at Sofievka near Kiev as tutor for his future wife, Olga Loyev.

1880   Forced to leave Sofievka; becomes "crown rabbi" of Loubny. First Hebrew writings appear in *Ha-Zefirah* and *Ha-Meliz.*

1881   Assassination of Alexander II followed by fierce pogroms and restrictive May Laws of 1882.

1883   Marries Olga Loyev; first Yiddish stories—"The Elections" and "Two Stones"—appear under the name Sholom Aleichem.

1887   Endowed at the death of his father-in-law, Sholom Aleichem moves to Kiev and establishes himself both as a businessman on the exchange and as a writer. "The Penknife."

1888   As a writer of fiction, as a critic, and as editor of the *Yidishe Folksbiblyotek,* Sholom Aleichem helps to launch modern Yiddish literature. The novels *Sender Blank, Yosele Solovey,* and *Stempenyu* written at this time.

1890   Financial failure halts publication of *Folksbiblyotek* after two annual issues; moves with growing family to the active literary community of Odessa.

1892   First letters of Menakhem-Mendl published.

1893   Return to Kiev; first of Tevye stories appears in the following year.

1897 First Zionist Congress at Basel; initiation of the Socialist Bund; upsurge of Yiddish journalism.

1901-
1903 Period of active writing includes many of his best-known stories: "The Little Pot," "The Fiddle, " "The Enchanted Tailor." Free to devote full time to writing after 1903, the year of the pogrom at Kishinev.

1905 Revolution followed by pogroms in many cities including Kiev.

1906 Sholom Aleichem leaves Russia for safety in western Europe and America, where his hopes as a playwright are disappointed; settles in Geneva in the following year.

1908 Collapse while on tour in August; analyzed as tuberculosis.

1909 International jubilee of fiftieth birthday and twenty-fifth year as a Yiddish writer. Convalescence and years of active writing. Most of the *Railway Stories,* additions to Menakehm-Mendl, Tevye and Mottel, and the novel· *Wandering Star* as well as several plays belong to this period.

1914 Return for what will be a last visit to Russia in successful reading tour; leaves Europe at war; arrives in New York in December.

1915 Contributes to Yiddish press in New York; begins his autobiography in earnest. His son Misha dies in Copenhagen.

1916 Sholom Aleichem dies on May 13; tribute of a massive funeral procession before burial at the cemetary Har Ha-Karmel in Brooklyn.

CHAPTER 1

Life and Times

SHORTLY before he died Sholom Aleichem wrote his autobiography, *Fun'm Yarid* (From the Fair). In the preface he says that he will record the story of his fifty years, but in fact he got no further than the age of twenty-one. The autobiography is the story of childhood and adolescence. It is also the story of several small towns, primarily Voronko, where he was raised, and of a country estate where he met the woman who would become his wife. If the autobiography tells nothing of his marriage and of the great cities where he lived—Kiev and Odessa, Geneva and New York—it is generally assumed that the whole story would have followed if only he had lived longer to finish writing it. But there is reason to believe that his prefatory promise of fifty years is a smokescreen for a life that was always to be remembered as a story of childhood and the story of a country town.

In 1895 when he first conceived of writing his autobiography, he wrote to M. Spektor: "Just as the best book is life itself and the best *roman* is life and my life is rich in various episodes and characters and types, I have decided to write my autobiography from birth to my twentieth year."[1] Although the project was dropped at that time and not taken up again until 1909 when it was dropped again, and not actually written until 1913, there is no reason to believe that his original plan had ever really changed. The autobiography was to be the story of a Jewish youth in the Russian Pale. Scenes of childhood are interspersed with portraits of small-town types, and the whole is uncluttered with specific facts, dates, names, and numbers of brothers and sisters. Voronko is initially introduced as "Kasrilevke," his fictional version of the typical *shtetl*. In his autobiography Sholom Aleichem creates for himself the typical life of his generation, a generation that saw the center of Jewish life shift from the small towns and villages of the Pale to crowded cities and to America. Whatever was to become of the people of this generation, they would retain the association of youth and the *shtetl*. The small town with its life regulated by religious tradition, subject to few intrusions from the outside world, would represent youth for millions of Jews. Pogroms and forced eviction, railroad trains, steamships, industrialized cities, and jerry-built tenements would appear in the 1880s to draw that generation *en masse* into the modern world. Up to that point the life of his generation would also be Sholom Aleichem's life. In addition to its typical activities, childhood would also be a time for the making of the future artist. The child is an observer, an imitator, a collector. His sensibility is touched in a way that puts him far enough outside the mainstream of small-town Jewish life to criticize it and to recognize its virtues and finally to record its passing.

I *Youth and the* Shtetl, *1859-1880*

Sholom Aleichem was raised in Voronko, but he was born nearby in the Ukrainian town of Pereyaslav, east of the Dnieper, on March 2, 1859. Two hundred years earlier the Ukrainian separatist Bogdan Chmielnitsky had signed a treaty with the Russian czar in Pereyaslav. Both opposed the dominance of the Polish overlords throughout the region. After twenty years of warfare another treaty signed at Androsovo (1667) finally divided the Ukraine on either side of the Dnieper. Kiev and Pereyaslav and the lands to the east fell to Russia. For the Jews of the Ukraine the time of Chmielnitsky was a catastrophe commonly referred to as "the deluge." Since many Jews served the Polish lords as agents, Chmielnitsky claimed all Jews to be the enemies of his Cossack soldiers whose tortures would be recalled during the pogroms of 1881. By Sholom Aleichem's time the name of Chmielnitsky had entered the local folklore of the towns and villages of the Ukraine.

In the two hundred years between Chmielnitsky's time and the birth of Sholom Aleichem all of the lands west of the Dnieper had fallen to Russia. By 1795 what remained of Poland had been divided among her neighbors. In the division Russia acquired the vast territories running north of the Ukraine to the Baltic and with it nearly a million Jews and a "Jewish Question" that would never be answered.

The Russian administration's Jewish policy from the first partition of Poland to the early 1880s was hesitant and vacillating; it either reversed itself constantly or moved in two different directions at the same time. On the one hand, efforts were made to "civilize" or "normalize" the Jewish population. . . . on the other hand, these attempts at "normalization" were superseded over and over again by measures designed to crush the "stubborn and recalcitrant lot" once and for all.[2]

Under Nicholas I (1825-1855) Jews were officially excluded from many villages and certain cities such as Kiev and further concentrated in the so-called Pale of Settlement, a territory that extends along what is now the entire western border of the Soviet Union. A series of restrictive laws passed in the 1820s and 1830s aimed at the normalization and eventual elimination of a distinct Jewish population. In the most extreme of these measures military service was made an instrument of aggressive repression. Jewish youth could be inducted any time after the age of twelve and kept in "cantonment" until they were eighteen when the mandatory twenty-five years of service began. Many did not survive, and more did not survive as Jews. In effect, Jewish education was offset or simply replaced by military training. Censorship of Jewish books was meant to have the same effect, and so was the seemingly benevolent institution of the "crown schools," which began to offer secular education to Jews in the 1840s. Nicholas' laws, especially military recruitment, tended to divide the Jewish community into the privileged and the unprivileged. Little was actually done to gratify the merchants and artisans, but they were largely exempt from the severity of military service which could usually be shunted onto the poor. Up to a point bribery could be used to circumvent other disabilities.

After 1855 and the debacle of Crimea the new czar, Alexander II, promoted policies that can be called enlightened insofar as they extended special privileges to "useful" Jews and equalized the burdens of the "useless" with those of the Gentile population. The czar who liberated the serfs also opened the interior of Russia and many previously restricted cities to Jews with commercial interests and educational qualifications. Quotas were enlarged in the universities. Jewish enlightenment was further encouraged by the relaxation of censorship and the consequent foundation of a Hebrew and Yiddish press. The Jewish enlightenment or *Haskalah* originated in Berlin at the end of the eighteenth century, and by the middle of the nineteenth century this diversified movement had impressed many Russian Jews with the value of a modern, secular education that would often include the study of Hebrew as a literary language. Whatever the specific form taken by the *Haskalah,* it promoted reform in Jewish education. The reformers—*maskilim,* as the enlightened ones were called—and positivists accepted the promise implied by Alexander's reforms in the 1860s, that they could at last lead lives as enlightened Jews and Russians. This was the world, apparently a new world, into which Sholom Aleichem was born.

His name was Sholom Nokhem Vevek's; that is, Sholom the son of Nokhem who was the son of Vevek. Officially the family bore the name Rabinovitsh, but in the small towns of the Pale it was enough to know the name of the parents, the father or the mother, and perhaps of the grandparents. Beyond the range where these names would be known, people rarely traveled. When Sholom was an infant the family moved to Voronko, which was not far away. In *Fun'm Yarid* he describes Voronko as a town like hundreds of other *shtetlakh,* with its old synagogue, its ritual bath, its large marketplace filled with shops and stalls where Jews conducted business with each other and with the peasants of the surrounding countryside, and its ancient cemetery in which the townspeople's ancestors lay buried, including the "dead from the ancient massacres of Chmielnitsky's time."

In Voronko, Nokhem Vevek's was considered a *nogid* — rich man and a leader of the community. He supplied beets to the sugar mill, freighted barges on the Dnieper, and, most important, he ran the rural post office and general store with his wife, Khaya Esther. Nokhem Vevek's was a pious man, a disciple of the Hasidic Rabbi of Talna as well as a Hebrew scholar and something of a *maskil.* He was a reader of the new, secular Hebrew literature such as the novels of Abraham Mapu, and he was prepared to give his son a modern education alongside the traditional one. Reb Nokhem bears little resemblance to the threatening, sour, sickly fathers in the stories.

The security and respectability of Voronko was not to last. Shortly before the boy's *bar mitzvah* his father suffered a financial fall, and the family, which Sholom Aleichem indiscriminately numbers at "about a dozen," was forced to move back to Pereyaslav. The sons stayed behind to finish the school year in *kheder,* and when they joined their parents they found them operating and inhabiting an inn. It was a poor inn, and the children were shocked to discover the loss of many valued objects, pawned and never redeemed. Khaya Esther fed them a meager meal and locked what remained in an otherwise empty cabinet. The children slept on straw. During the summer following Shalom's *bar mitzvah* a cholera epidemic broke out in the town. While his father joined the society of *reybers,* those who massage or rub the victims, his mother was stricken and died. Suddenly in the course of a year, the year in which he technically passed into Jewish manhood, the security and the comfort of his early years were lost. According to the definition of the term in the *shtetl,* Sholom was suddenly a *yossem* ("orphan") and very nearly a pauper. The trials of that year would survive in dozens of stories about orphanage and loss. The adult writer, later haunted by his own bankruptcy, the loss of furniture, and the dispersion of his family, would recall and recreate the moment of adolescent insecurity.

Young Sholom was not an orphan for long. His father went to Berdichev, "the place where most stepmothers come from," to find a new wife, and he came back with a classical example. Under the orders of his *shtifmuter* Sholom was obliged to sit out in the road and solicit lodgers who rarely stopped. Any tasks that did not advance the precarious prosperity of the inn were considered a waste of time. Thanks to the sharp tongue that she used to enforce her discipline Sholom acquired a rich vocabulary of Yiddish maledictions. These he collected in a little anthology which constitutes his first Yiddish writing. When his father caught him at this work, Sholom expected the worst, but the father was amused and so, oddly enough, was the stepmother, who was otherwise not pleased by literary exercises. His stepmother's robust use of the language and the time spent at the crossroads watching the world go by were an excellent apprenticeship for the Yiddish *folks-shrayber.*

At about the same time, when Sholom was fifteen, he read the popular historical novel *Ahavath Tsiyon (The Love of Zion),* by Abraham Mapu. For many young men in the Pale *The Love of Zion* was a first novel, read secretly between the pages of the *Gemarah.* In Nokhem Vevek's home the reading of a Hebrew novel was encouraged, and when Sholom set out to write an imitation, *Bas Tsiyon (The Daughter of Zion),* his father was delighted and showed the work to the friends who regularly gathered there. The life of the writer had begun significantly between the elaborate, biblical Hebrew of Mapu and the earthy, quotidian Yiddish of his stepmother.

By that time the family's economic situation had improved slightly—they had left the inn for a wine and tobacco shop—and attention could be given to the young man's education. In Voronko all of the boys had been taught in *kheder* by Reb Zorakh'l, the *melamed*. The *kheder* was conducted in the single room of the hut "on chicken legs" where Reb Zorakh'l lived and where his wife, with the help of her husband's pupils, cooked, and tended her own children. In the center of the room was a long table with benches where the scholars sat and chanted, or rather shouted, their lessons in unison. The *melamed's* chief aid was a *kantchik* ("small whip"). Beatings, pinches, and slaps were the regular companions of such an education. Here Sholom learned to read Hebrew and acquired the rudiments of Russian grammar and arithmetic. One of the chief accomplishments he derived from Reb Zorakh'l was a fine handwriting in Hebrew. In a sense he was a calligrapher before he was a writer.

When the family moved back to Pereyaslav he was enrolled in a Russian school over the objections of his pious uncles. It was understood that the Russian schools in the time of the moderately enlightened Czar Alexander set out to "normalize" their Jewish students, but Nokhem was able to arrange for his son to avoid classes in Christian religion and to maintain his own religious studies while receiving a decent secular education. All of this was to prepare him for the Jewish Teachers' Institute at Zhitomir, which had recently taken the place of the famous rabbinic academy. But in 1874 Alexander had reformed military service to equalize requirements and reduce the obligation to six years. As Simon Dubnow has pointed out, this "was the first act to equalize Jews in duties before they were granted equal rights."[3] Dubnow, the great historian of the Jews in Russia and later a friend of Sholom Aleichem, is generally skeptical of Alexander's reforms. In this case, they kept Sholom out of the institute at Zhitomir, because school authorities decided that, since he would become eligible for the army in the fall of 1880, he would not be able to finish his education which would require still another year. Thus ended the formal education of the writer. In that world he had already gone far. Except during the brief relaxation of restrictions in the 1860s and 1870s few Jews could expect to enter Russian universities, and as a result some of the most learned Jews of the Pale—Dubnow himself, and Ahad Ha'am— were self-taught.

For Sholom Rabinovitsh this meant that he was in the world and obliged to earn a living sooner than he had expected. He had already moved away from home to a room where he could give his time to study, free from the distractions of his own home and the eye of his stepmother. He earned his board giving *shtundes* ("hours")—that is, lessons—to the children of his landlord, and for extra money he gave lessons to other children and some adults. After the disappointment of Zhitomir he left Pereyaslav, first to seek a job in the household of a *nogid* in a nearby town. When that plan failed he found himself quite by chance on the estate of one Elimelekh Loyev. At the inn where he had been staying while he failed to get the original job he met Loyev's son, Yeshia, who knew that his father was seeking a tutor for the daughter of his second marriage. Elimelekh Loyev appeared, examined the young man, and took him to his estate at Sofievka in the province of Kiev, where he would stay for the three most comfortable years of his life. In this fine country house he had a room of his own that opened out on gardens where he would walk and talk with his young pupil after the lessons of the morning. Olga Loyev was thirteen years old when Sholom arrived and sixteen when he left. The parents were busy, and the young people walked and talked and read and eventually fell in love, though at the time they did not acknowledge their attachment. Together they read the Russian classics as well as translations from German, French, and English, and at night Sholom was free to write. Later he would refer to "long, heart-rending novels, melodramatic plays, complicated tragedies and comedies" written in that period, but nothing survives.[4] In any case this writing would not have been in Yiddish. That would wait.

When he was not teaching, reading, writing, or courting, Sholom served as secretary for Elimelekh Loyev. Loyev leased his land from two noblemen, surpervised all the activities of the farm, and conducted the sale of grain and sugar beets. The peasants who worked the land still bore the scars on their bodies from the whippings they had received as serfs. Sholom was to find that a world of Jews who owned or leased land and employed workers who respected them was not uncommon at that time. "It is hard to imagine," he would write in his autobiography, "what course Jewish history might have taken and what role we might have played in the economic and political life of the country if it were not for Ignatiev."[5] Ignatiev was the primary author of the "Temporary Regulations," which severly limited Jewish ownership of land after May, 1882. But before the so-called May Laws would come the assassination of Alexander II and the terrible pogroms of 1881, and before that Sholom would be obliged to leave his temporary paradise at Sofievka.

The first reason for leaving Sofievka was the draft. His time came, and it was necessary to go to the neighboring town of Kaniev, where, through the intercession of Loyev, his papers had been moved. There his protector's influence was sufficient to release him from service. But shortly after his return, when the attachment of student and teacher was discovered, the protection ceased. What offended the father was the secrecy of the love rather than Sholom's poverty. Forced to leave, Sholom went immediately to the capital of the province, Kiev, which was to become "Yehupetz," the geographical center of his fictional world. Jews were not allowed to reside in Kiev without a special permit. These permits were granted to skilled artisans, merchants of the first guild, and *Nikolaevske soldaty*, soldiers who had served the twenty-five-year term under Nicholas. There was no place for a young writer without *protektzia* ("influence"). A series of inquiries led him to the nearby town of Belaya Tserkov, where he was cheated out of what money he had by a *vinkel advokat*, a corner lawyer, who had supposedly hired him as a secretary. Left penniless, Sholom wrote to his father in Pereyaslav. Nokhem responded with money and advice. The position of "crown rabbi" was opening for election in the town of Loubny. The task and status of the crown rabbi (*rabbiner*) are best described in a story that Sholom Aleichem was to write many years later:

Once I was a rabbiner. A rabbiner, not a rabbi. That is, I was called a rabbi but a rabbi of the crown. To old country Jews I don't have to explain what a rabbi of the crown is. They know the breed. What are his great responsibilities? He fills out birth certificates, officiates at circumcisions, performs marriages, grants divorces. He gets his share from the living and the dead. In the synagogue he has a place of honor, and when the congregation rises, he is the first to stand. On legal holidays he appears in a stovepipe hat and holds forth in his best Russian: *"Gospoda Prihozhane!"* To take it for granted that among our people a rabbiner is well loved—let's not say any more. Say rather that we put up with him, as we do a government inspector or a deputy sheriff. And yet he is chosen from among the people, that is, every three years a proclamation is sent us: *"Na Osnavania Predpisania. . . ."* Or, as we would say: "Your Lord, the Governor, orders you to come together in the synagogue, poor little Jews, and pick out a rabbiner for yourselves. . . ."[6]

In this case Sholom had *protektzia* and got the job. As it happened, the former crown rabbi of Loubny had been a young man from Pereyaslav, and many of his old townsmen resented the intervention. Sholom's ascent to a position of questionable merit was touched with shame. His vow to be a humane *rabbiner* is the conclusion of his autobiography, and a satire written in Yiddish about the election process was the first publication to bear the name "Sholom Aleichem."

Although he would remain in Loubny for three years and then return to Belaya Tserkov and Sofievka, his life in the *shtetl* essentially ended with his first trip to Kiev. Circumstances propelled him into an urban world of business and literature at a time when Jews all over Russia were entering a period of great difficulty and rapid change. Sholom Aleichem became a writer in the time of the "Temporary Regulations" which were still in effect thirty-five years later at the time of his death.

II *Another Deluge and a New Culture*

The years of Sholom Aleichem's literary development began with another "deluge" comparable to the assault on Jews in Chmielnitsky's time. The assassination of Alexander II in March, 1881, initiated a series of terrible pogroms especially virulent in the province of Kiev and the neighboring provinces of Podolia and Volhynia. The city of Kiev was the site of bloody and destructive riots in April. A second wave of pogroms in July was especially harsh in the towns such as Pereyaslav to which fugitives from Kiev had fled. Pogroms were encouraged by deliberate policy at every level of government. As long as they were sanctioned from above these "spontaneous" riots continued. Soon, however, they were replaced by what Dubnow calls a period of "legislative pogroms" initiated by the "Temporary Regulations" of May, 1882. The effect of the May Laws was to increasingly restrict Jewish settlement to the already overcrowded cities. Jews were not allowed to settle or purchase property outside the cities and towns. Since the rules were not retroactive, Jews living in the villages at that time could not be evicted. Laws passed during the next two decades would bite into that population. Towns could be declared villages and thereby be put off limits for Jews already settled. A Jew who left his village for a certain length of time could return home to find himself labeled a new settler and subject to eviction. Cities like Rostov-on-Don and Taganrog were arbitrarily excluded from the Pale just as the czar's summer retreat at Yalta was voided of its nonresident Jews in 1893. Alexander died before he could enjoy his newly purged resort, but Nicholas II continued the repressive policies of the previous regime. Jews were further removed from the countryside by the removal of a major source of income when the government assumed monopoly of the liquor trade in 1894. Suddenly several hundred thousand Jews involved in the production and distribution of liquor found themselves without income. Twenty years earlier Sholom Aleichem's father had taken recourse to innkeeping and winemaking when his previous business failed. This would not have been possible under the new laws.

Had there been alternative ways of making a living, the government assumption of the liquor concession might be looked upon as a wholesome reform that relieved Jews of the onus of supplying drink to their hostile neighbors. But thanks to the May Laws the countryside was closed to Jews for purposes of agriculture and little was done to encourage Jewish artisans. Jews could not expect advancement in the army or entry into the civil service. Movement in other directions was limited by the small ratio of Jews allowed into Russian gymnasia and universities. Although Jews frequently constituted more than half the population of towns in the Pale, room was only made for 10 percent in the gymnasia and in the universities. Outside the Pale universities would receive 5 percent, and in St. Petersburg and Moscow 3 percent. These quotas were further reduced in 1901. Sholom Aleichem's play *Shver tsu zayn a yid (It's Hard to be a Jew)* begins with the complaint of a Jewish student whose gold medal at the gymnasium will not get him into the university. Many of these frustrated students were sent abroad for further education and would feed the cadres of revolutionary exiles. If a Jew were to succeed in attaining an education within

Russia, there was very little that could be done with it afterward. Typical of the restraint placed on professional life was the law of 1889 requiring permission from the minister of justice for a lawyer of "non-Christian denominations" to enter the bar. In the next five years no Jew received this permission.

Academic and professional restrictions only scratch the surface of the burdens placed on the Jewish population of Russia. The commission of Count Pahlen, appointed to propose new legislation in 1883, studied 650 anti-Jewish laws before it recommended the emancipation and consequent assimilation of the Jews. By 1897 that population had risen to nearly six million, and K. P. Pobedonostsev, who had rejected the proposals of the Pahlen Commission a decade earlier, made his own grim prediction: "One-third will die out, one-third will leave the country, and one-third will be completely dissolved in the surrounding population."[7] What Pobedonostsev foresaw was the total disappearance of the Jews from Russia, and this was the apparent goal of all the legal machinery aimed at them. The Jew was made invisible, unseen by the peasant in the countryside, unseen by the czar in Yalta, unseen among jurists, doctors, or professors. Jews were systematically excluded from the mainstream of Russian life. So too were poor Russians, but Jews were distinguished further as aliens (*inorodtsy*) and separated from the "indigenous" population. It is no wonder that one-third of the Jews in Russia should choose to alienate themselves totally through emigration during the four decades that followed the pogroms of 1881. Another third was kept perpetually on the edge of starvation and very nearly fulfilled that part of the ministerial prophecy. Sometimes up to half of a given community would appeal for relief at Passover time. If wholesale conversion and assimilation did not absorb those Jews who remained in Russia, it was largely because of new movements that strengthened national self-consciousness in the face of external humiliation.

After 1881 the Jewish intelligentsia knew what it could expect from the apparently benign offer of Russification made by the previous regime and from the promises of populist revolutionaries. The Left stood by while the Right encouraged the pogroms and made new laws. For many Jews emigration was the first response and America the obvious goal. A much smaller faction looked to Palestine. M. L. Lilienblum, who had begun his public life as a critic of Jewish education from the point of view of *Haskalah* and then of positivism, was among the first to give his attention to Palestine. Only there would Jews cease to be aliens. Dr. Leon Pinsker developed similar ideas in his pamphlet *Auto-Emancipation* (1882). No longer should Jews rely on the gift of civic emancipation; rather, they should act on their own to restore their rights as a group in one location. Zionism developed slowly in Russia until it was bolstered from the West by the ideological support of Theodor Herzl, whose first Zionist Congress of 1897 gave shape to a broad political movement. Even after the ascendancy of Herzl, Zionism in Russia retained a strong cultural or spiritual flavor given it by Ahad Ha'am. Ahad Ha'am saw Palestine as a center of Jewish culture which could give guidance to the great number of Jews obliged for the time being to remain in the diaspora. Simon Dubnow foresaw "national rejuvenation in Russia itself," where Jews should seek "national-cultural autonomy."[8] Even Jewish socialists, historically committed to internationalism and class interest, began to require autonomy by 1905, a position that alienated the *Bund* from much of the Russian left.

These diverse movements all had one thing in common. At some point all aimed at what Dubnow calls "national rejuvenation upon modern foundations," and at some point all appealed to the vernacular as a language of political and literary discourse in the Pale. For Dubnow Yiddish was the language of the national-cultural revival, a language ennobled by its dominant usage in the current phase of Jewish history. Zionists who favored Hebrew were obliged to speak Yiddish to the Jewish masses, and socialists who may have favored Russian were equally obliged to speak to Jewish workers in their own language. The elevation of Yiddish as the key to new power in the social and political spheres coincided with its elevation as a literary language.

The career of the Yiddishist Nokhum Shtif (1879-1933) is instructive. Shtif, a son of middle-class parents in Rovno, Volhynia (the province just west of Kiev), was given an excellent education according to the lights of *Haskalah*. He studied Hebrew with a private tutor and read the Bible beyond the conventional five books as well as modern Hebrew writers. At fifteen he was enrolled in a public *Realschule,* the equivalent to the gymnasium devoted to modern scientific studies. At eighteen he became an ardent Zionist after the first Congress at Basel. A year later he moved to Kiev, where he was enrolled in the Polytechnikum and there associated himself with socialists. His radicalism advanced with the pogroms of 1903, and he assisted in the foundation of the Jewish Socialist Labor Party, the Seymists. A year later he was found with a volume of Lenin under his pillow. He was arrested, released, expelled from the Polytechnikum, and ultimately found himself with many other young Russians in exile in Switzerland. During this time he had become a Yiddishist. Although he had always heard Yiddish at home, he had been convinced by his Russian education that he did not know the language. His first serious exposure was through the Zionists: "I first heard about Yiddish in a serious vein when Sholom Aleichem read his stories at Zionist gatherings in Kiev in 1900-02." Several years later at Bern he found "Yiddish propaganda" among the papers of the Yiddishist and socialist Chaim Zhitlowsky, along with "the Bund's underground literature." Shtif was exposed to Yiddish by two movements that were willing to use the vernacular in order to reach the populace, but as a result of his exposure he came to see "Yiddish as a culture, not merely as a tool to enlighten the masses." He became an active literary critic, a historian of the language, and one of the founders of the Yiddish Scientific Institute (YIVO).[9]

As we have seen, the new political movements gave a platform for the advancement of Yiddish literature. In addition to the public readings, they supported newspapers and journals where the works of the Yiddish writers would appear in print. Beyond that the new movements imbued Yiddish literature with a strong sense of social justice and injustice within the Jewish world and in the world at large.

The pogrom policy of the Russian government after 1881 forced Jews to redefine their position in the diaspora. One effect of aggressive official policy coincided with the general effect of modernization—Jews were being forced more and more into the cities. In the nineteenth century urbanization generally went hand in hand with industrialization, though in Russia nascent industry could not keep up with the concentration of labor in the Pale. Modern transportation which brought Jews to the cities also brought them to the borders and abroad. Russian policy accelerated urbanization and emigration and changed the base of Jewish life in Russia at a time when traditional religious practice and traditional folkways were giving way to the advancement of science and industry all over western Europe and America as well as

in Russia and among Jews. In this multiform process Yiddish was
to play an important role. Among Jews it was both the language of
the vanishing folklore and of the new masses. It was precisely at
this point, at the beginning of the 1880s, that Sholom Aleichem
began to write Yiddish stories that would transport the folk voice
into the modern world.

III *The Writer in the City: Kiev and Odessa, 1880–1905*

Little is known about the period of the rabbinate, those three
years that follow the cessation of the autobiography and precede
the publication of his first Yiddish stories. It is known that he wrote
several Hebrew essays on the subject of Jewish education for the
Hebrew weeklies *Ha-Zefirah* and *Ha-Meliz*. A cousin of Olga
Loyev who saw these articles written under the name of Sholom
Rabinovitsh brought about the reunion of the young people. They
were married in Kiev on May 12, 1883, without the knowledge of
Elimelekh Loyev. However, the father was soon reconciled with his
daughter and prevailed upon his son-in-law to give up his position
in Loubny and return to Sofievka. After a summer at the old
establishment the couple took up residence in Belaya Tserkov,
where Sholom worked briefly for the sugar magnate, Brodsky,
before Loyev again intervened and offered support. Such aid was
not uncommon, but it was generally used to sponsor Talmudic
study and not Yiddish writing. For by 1883 Sholom Rabinovitsh
had become Sholom Aleichem, a writer of Yiddish.

The pseudonym first appeared as a camouflage for the author of
"Di Vibores" ("The Elections"), a satire of the way the rich men
of a certain small town fix the election of their rabbiner. The name
was also a useful cover for a young writer who was trying his hand
at what was still a questionable pursuit, the writing of Yiddish. In
this case the name which was to assure anonymity also made the
author a man of the people whose name—the conventional
greeting, "Peace be with you"—was already a household word.[10]

When Sholom Aleichem's first Yiddish stories and satires appeared, few serious Jewish writers deigned to use what was called
"jargon." Even five years later when, as editor of *Di Yidishe
Folksbiblyotek,* Sholom Aleichem invited a contribution from the
Hebrew poet, Y. L. Gordon, he received a wary response:

You ask my opinion of the jargon. I have always thought the speech of our people to be in the same sad state as their history. . . . I marvel at you. You write Russian fluently and you are a master of our literary language, Hebrew. How can you give yourself up to cultivating the jargon?[11]

Modern Yiddish literature was, in fact, about as old as Sholom Aleichem. In 1862, encouraged by the recent relaxation of censorship, Alexander Tseyderboym began to publish a Yiddish supplement to the Hebrew *Ha-Meliz*. This supplement, *Kol Mevasser* —"The voice which brings tidings" (Isa. 52:7)—helped to standardize printed Yiddish in its reports on Jewish news and culture, and it stimulated the writing of Yiddish fiction for a decade. There was a Yiddish literature before the 1860s, but the new writers found in it little inspiration. Biblical redactions and translations, homiletic books and prayers written for women who were seldom taught Hebrew came out of the sixteenth century and were still in use in the nineteenth. Folktales and romances had been borrowed from various host cultures. Primitive dramas written for the holidays, expecially Purim, were still performed, as well as plays based on the lives of biblical heroes and performed by schoolchildren. More recently the hagiography of the hasidic movement, primarily stories about its leader, the Baal Shem Tov (ca. 1700-1760), came down to later generations in the language of the people to whom he made his appeal. The tales of the hasidic Rabbi Nachman of Bratslav (1770-1811), recorded by his disciples, were also widely read. At first this existent literature was not enough for the young writers though later they would make valuable discoveries, especially of the hasidic lore. Still as late as 1910 Y. L. Peretz, who by that time had begun to publish his own versions of hasidic tales, would still describe Yiddish literature as a literature without a tradition. "Our orphan-children wear the old clothes of strangers."[12]

The fortune of Elimelekh Loyev, put at the disposal of his new son-in-law, was destined to help clothe the new literature with its own ready-made traditions. Loyev died in 1885, and since the sons of his first marriage had both died before him, the estate and a considerable inheritance fell to Sholom and Olga. They quickly liquidated the estate and moved to Kiev with their firstborn daughter, Ernestina, and Loyev's widow, Rachel, called "Babushka"—grandma. In Kiev Sholom Aleichem wrote his first novels—*Sender Blank, Yosele Solovey,* and *Stempenyu*—as well as numerous short stories. From the point of view of the new literature, his publication of the *Yidishe Folksbiblyotek* at the end of the decade was of greater service than his own early fiction. He was able to publish this annual in 1888 and 1889 at his own expense with his inheritance and with the income that he drew off the Kiev bourse. One function of the *Folksbiblyotek* was to canonize recent Yiddish writers in their own tradition. Dan Miron describes the way this process began in the critical essays that Sholom Aleichem was writing for several years before the publication of the annual:

The air of a well-established literary tradition and of a lively literary milieu is conveyed in every one of these articles. Writers are treated in them not only as if they were known and accepted as grand public figures but also as if their places in a literary hierarchy had been long recognized and agreed upon.[13]

The primary position in this tradition was given to the man whom Sholom Aleichem was to call *zeyde* ("grandfather"), S. Y. Abramovitsh (1836-1917), who had been writing Yiddish fiction since the mid-1860s under the name of Mendele Moykher-Sforim, Mendele the Book-Peddler. Also canonized, though with slightly inferior epithets, were A. M. Dik (1814-1893), Y. Y. Linetski (1839-1915), and the playwright Abraham Goldfaden (1840-1908). These writers were elevated not so much in contradistinction to the old storybooks as to new writers of *shund* ("trash"). Chief among these was N. M. Shaykevitsh (1849-1905), whose sentimental romances with their inevitably happy endings were seen to be corrupting the taste of Yiddish readers. In *Shomers Mishpet (The Trial of Shomer,* referring to the pen name of the author) Sholom Aleichem castigated the *romanmakher* ("novel-maker") and in the same year, 1888, published the first volume of the *Folksbiblyotek* as a forum for the worthy writers of Yiddish, old and new. Mendele contributed an expanded version of his early novel *Dos Vintshfingerl (The Magic Ring)*; Linetski, whose *Dos Poylishe Yingel* (The Polish Boy, 1867) enjoyed great popularity, contributed *Der Vorim in der Khreyn (The Worm in the Horseradish).* Sholom Aleichem also encouraged contributions from people who had barely written in Yiddish before. The skeptical Y.L. Gordon was published here along with the first Yiddish publication of Y. L.

Peretz, a long ballad called "Monish." Sholom Aleichem's own novel, *Stempenyu,* was published as a supplement to the first volume with an elaborate dedicatory letter addressed to the "grandfather," Mendele.

Sholom Aleichem met Mendele for the first time in Odessa in 1888 and again in 1890. They were to remain close friends as long as they lived. Although in this ready-made tradition the grandfather of Yiddish literature was only twenty-three years older than the grandson, Sholom Aleichem liked to play Dante to the older man's Virgil. In time it was necessary for the younger writer to wriggle out of the filial role, a process which Sholom Aleichem describes in an amusing anecdote written twenty years later in an essay called "Auto-da-fé." Sholom Aleichem recalls that he had just written a novel in the allegorical style of Mendele's *Di Kliatche (The Nag,* 1873) in which the Jewish people are compared to the worn-out old mare. After he heard the first part of his friend's novel, Mendele asked if there was a fire lit in the kitchen. Was he hungry, asked his young friend. No, said Mendele, the fire would be for the manuscript. As Sholom Aleichem's son-in-law Y. D. Berkovitsh has written: "Under Mendele's influence, Sholom Aleichem freed himself from Mendele's influence."[14]

In the Odessa writing colony Mendele had detractors as well as admirers. At the head of the opposition was Linetski, who liked to think of himself as the elder statesman of Yiddish writers. To him Sholom Aleichm was "a rich young man" who amused himself editing an annual and patronizing Yiddish writers. At the same time he complained that he was paid too little for his contribution to the *Folksbiblyotek.* Shortly before the first issue of Sholom Aleichem's annual a Yiddish journal called *Der Hoyz-fraynt (The Housefriend)* appeared in St. Petersburg under the editorship of M. Spektor, another early promotor of Yiddish literature. Spektor was to become a valued friend of Sholom Aleichem, but at this time they found themselves in competition. The group headed by Linetski put on a celebration in Odessa at which they praised *Der Hoyz-fraynt* and heaped scorn upon the *Folksbiblyotek* and chiefly on the self-appointed "grandfather" and "grandson" of Yiddish letters.

Sholom Aleichem responded with a banquet of his own given in Mendele's honor at the finest hotel in Odessa in the summer of 1890. This banquet lived in the memory of Yiddish writers for years afterward. The younger and still unknown writers crowded outside and peered in through the windows while inside one speaker after another heralded the flowering of Yiddish folk literature. Mendele himself spoke. Toward dawn M. L. Lilienblum, then secretary of the Jewish Burial Society, rose and exclaimed, "Ai, ai, it's day already. Time to go out and bury a few Jews."[15] A few more, he meant. In Yiddish as in Russian "to bury" someone is to heap scorn upon him. A new literature was born at these burials.

Lilienblum worked at the Burial Society; Mendele at the Talmud Toreh; Peretz was a lawyer who served the Jewish Burial Society in Warsaw. Very few Yiddish writers made a living from literature in 1890. Sholom Aleichem had recently inherited financial security, and, as we have seen, that security would allow him to promote Yiddish literature through the publication of his annual and at his banquets. The *Yidishe Folksbiblyotek* made two annual appearances but not a third. There would be no more banquets. In 1890 financial failure on the bourse drove the family from Kiev to Odessa; a second and more definitive collapse drove them back to Kiev in 1893, where for the next twelve years Sholom Aleichem led the busy life of a broker and a writer.

The picture that we have of the writer during these years is of a man who wrote standing or walking, indoors and out, sitting in railway carriages, in swaying wagons, and in restaurants around the bourse waiting for friends. Wherever he went he carried a small narrow notebook of his own construction that fitted the palm of his hand. At home he wrote standing at a high desk, also of his own design. He clearly enjoyed the physical act of writing. Y. D. Berkovitsh, who knew him later, describes his attachment to the desk, to the notebook, to his collection of colored pencils and inks, his scissors, binders, pasting materials, transparent gummed papers, and various sheets of paper of different colors and sizes.

The amount that he was actually able to write while recouping his financial losses in the early 1890s was limited, but it is to these years that the initiation of his finest works belongs. From his careful observation of the *luftmenshen* ("men of air," that is, men who live on air) who gathered about the bourse came the first of the Menakhem-Mendl letters (1892). The original Tevye—a man with no daughters—delivered milk to the summer residents of Boyarka (Boyberik in the stories), where the family spent its vacations in those years. In the early Tevye stories which began to appear in

1894, Tevye meets his kinsman Menakhem-Mendl, but after a financial crash which matches that of their maker these two figures would lead separate lives in stories written, edited, and collected over the course of the next twenty years.

By the end of the 1890s Sholom Aleichem's private financial condition had begun to improve. At the same time Yiddish literature was expanding under the influence of the new Zionist and Bundist activities that were accelerated with the official formation of both movements in 1897. New publications appeared in St. Petersburg and Warsaw. In the new press and especially in the Yiddish Zionist newspaper *Der Yid* Sholom Aleichem was a regular and successful contributor. His stories became required reading for a massive Jewish population who often bought them in little pamphlets for five kopeks as part of the supplies for a complete sabbath. The next several years were among his most productive. He created Kasrilevke in "Di shtodt fun di kleyne menshelekh" ("The Town of Little People," 1901), "Dos naye Kasrilevke" ("New Kasrilevke," 1901), and "Dreyfus in Kasrilevke" (1902). He also wrote "Der ferkishufter shnayder" ("The Enchanted Tailor," 1900) and the early monologues, "Dos Tepl" ("The Little Pot," 1901) and "Genz" ("Geese," 1902) as well as a number of his children's stories including "Oyf'n fidl" ("The Fiddle," 1902).

At last in 1903 Sholom Aleichem was able to quit his business life and devote himself entirely to writing. His new freedom was brief. At Kishinev, not far from Kiev, a deadly and destructive pogrom broke out in the spring of 1903. Kiev itself was struck in 1905. Jews found themselves caught in the middle of war, revolution, and counterrevolution in a period of turmoil that Sholom Aleichem would describe in a novel called at different times *Der Mabl (The Deluge)* and *In Shturm (In the Storm)*. By 1906 it had become impossible for him to continue to live and write in Kiev. He and his family began the journey that a million Russian Jews had already made since 1880. They set out for America.

IV *Exile, 1906–1916*

Modern critics have come to regard exile, spiritual or political, as a natural condition of the artist. For Jewish writers, displaced by czarist Russia, exile had several meanings. A Jew in Russia was constantly reminded of his alien status. The conditions imposed by the Russian government only reinforced the Jewish sense of an exile that began with the destruction of the second Temple and would end only with the coming of the Messiah and return to the Land of Israel. Zionists proposed the political replacement of exile with settlement in Palestine. The so-called *galut* ("Diaspora") nationalists proposed national and cultural consolidation in the various centers where Jews found themselves living outside Palestine. All agreed that they lived in exile. But Jews had been exiled in Poland and Russia for a long time, and for many the further shift westward must be seen as a second exile. Sholom Aleichem was one of these.

Sholom Aleichem was a Russian. Russian was the language spoken at home, and when the family began to travel, Russian tutors had to be found for the children. His son Misha remained in Kiev as long as possible to pursue his education; the education of the daughters presupposed return. As a writer his strongest affiliations were, of course, with Russian Jews whose company he continued to keep in the émigré communities of western Europe and America. At the same time he continued to read the Russians. With Tolstoy and Chekhov he had corresponded briefly after Kishinev; Gorki he met once. Through the frequent illness and insomnia of his exile he encouraged his daughters to read to him from Chekhov's stories, and for years he had filled his little notebooks with passages from Gogol.

There was also the land. Sholom Aleichem's adult life was spent in great cities: Kiev, Odessa, Geneva, New York. What he knew of the land was the Ukrainian countryside remembered from his youth and later from the summers in Boyarka. The Hebrew poet, Bialik, also a Ukrainian, once said that while reading Sholom Aleichem's "Page from the Song of Songs" he could smell the odor of *Erev-Pesakh,* Passover eve, in the Ukrainian countryside. The two men were to meet in the Hague at the Zionist Conference of 1907. A famous photograph taken in Geneva later in the same year shows Mendele, Sholom Aleichem, the Russian-Jewish writer Ben Ami, and Bialik posed as if on a boating expedition in a photographer's studio. The four look curiously detached from the artificial setting. Sholom Aleichem stands behind the others with a straw hat thrown back on his head, a small and clearly useless oar in his right hand. All four look superimposed on a scene where they do not belong, four writers in exile.

For Sholom Aleichem the journey to America began where it

began for thousands of Jews from the south of Russia, in the Austro-Hungarian town of Brody. His expectation that money would come from America to support the rest of the journey was not immediately fulfilled. This would be the first of Sholom Aleichem's troubles with the Yiddish press and theater of New York which in various ways had promised sponsorship. On his own he was not without resources. Before leaving Russia he had begun reading tours which were especially popular with socialist and Zionist audiences. Now he would find himself equally popular in the cities and towns of Galicia among ardent hasidim as well as among the Germanized burghers. His readings carried him all over Rumania and into western Europe, eventually to Paris and London. By the summer of 1906 he could move his family to Geneva and continue on the American trip which was made in that year with his wife and young son Numa.

When Sholom Aleichem arrived in New York in October, 1906, he was met by a large delegation including Jewish intellectuals and jurists, Zionists, socialists, religious leaders, and, most important, representatives of the Yiddish press and theater. These last were to be his resources in the United States. The auspices were good. Immediately a reception and a banquet at Jacob Adler's Grand Theater yielded the famous if apocryphal compliment from Mark Twain—"I understand that I am the American Sholom Aleichem"—and a thousand dollars which he used to support one half of his family in Geneva and establish the other half in the Bronx.

First he gave his attention to the theater. Adler took *Samuel Pasternak,* a play based on chicanery at the Kiev bourse. To Boris Thomashefsky he gave a dramatization of *Stempenyu.* Both plays opened on February 8, 1907. The first audiences were enthusiastic, but reviews were mixed. The *Tageblatt* and the *Morgen Journal,* representing a middle-class religious community, praised both plays, but socialist and labor papers, *Forverts* and *Varheit,* found fault. The reviews reveal less about the plays than about the rivalries within the Jewish community. In this case labor won, and the plays both closed within two weeks.

Although he was able to make arrangements with *Varheit* and the *Tageblatt* to publish new writings, the pay was poor and the maintenance of a family on both sides of the Atlantic became impossible. When he left New York in June, 1907, his novel *Der mabl* along with several Tevye stories and parts of *Mottel, Peyse dem khazns (Mottel, son of Peyse the Cantor)* were running in the New York newspapers. Reestablished in Geneva, he sent stories and plays to newspapers in New York and Warsaw. A play, *Der oytser (The Treasure),* was rejected in New York. It was not until after his death with the rise of the Yiddish art theater in New York and Moscow that Sholom Aleichem's plays as well as dramatizations of his stories and novels would attain appropriate staging and consistently appreciative audiences.

The need for money had been a necessarily dominant motive from the time of his first financial failure in 1890. Although he was read throughout the Yiddish-speaking world, most of his readers bought pirated editions, and very little of the profit from reprints ever reached the author. In 1908, pressed again by need, he launched a reading tour in Poland and Russia. From Warsaw he embarked on a long series of one-night stands in the towns and cities of the Pale. In August he was engaged to appear in the town of Baranovitsh in Minsk Province. The young people of the town had planned this meeting, and the hall was crowded while many stood outside. He gave the announced readings and additional readings, but he was exhausted throughout. Afterward in his hotel he collapsed and suffered a pulmonary hemorrhage. His illness was diagnosed as tuberculosis and he was forced to remain in Baranovitch through the end of September, when he left to take up winter residence in the milder climate of the Italian Riviera at Nervi. Summers brought his dispersed family together. The reunions were happy, but work was slow.

It was only now, during this time of fragile health and enforced rest, that Sholom Aleichem became a financially independent writer. During the first year of his illness friends in the Warsaw literary community—Spektor and Jacob Dinesohn—called the attention of the Yiddish reading public to the essential penury of their favorite writer. With new support, the writer's wife, Olga, was able to go to Warsaw and successfully bargain for the rights to royalties. At the same time friends throughout the community of Yiddish writers and readers, now dispersed throughout the world, organized a jubilee that would coincide with Sholom Aleichem's fiftieth birthday and his twenty-fifth year as a Yiddish writer. Observance of the Sholom Aleichem Jubilee throughout the Yiddish-speaking world was also the observance of a broad cultural phenomenon which had been born with him and which had matured with him. It was as much the particular writer as the representative of a collective movement that was the subject of celebration. The Jubilee drew the attention of the world beyond the Yiddish community. Publication of authorized volumes in Warsaw was followed by translation into Russian. Sholom Aleichem had always wished to see his works translated into Russian; he was now pleased to assist in the project, and he was especially gratified by the praise of Russian critics.

It was after the "first meeting with the Angel of Death," as he called the illness that made him a semi-invalid from 1909 to 1913, that Sholom Aleichem seriously undertook the writing of the autobiography. He began to write in 1909, dropped the project, and recommenced in 1913 when a benefactor in Lausanne offered to publish the autobiography at his own expense. By that time parts had already appeared in the Hebrew journal *Ha-Tsefira* translated by Y. D. Berkovitsh. When the benefactor left Lausanne, Sholom Aleichem dropped the project once again and took it up finally at the end of his life, in New York. Between relapses of his tubercular condition in the years from 1909 to 1913, Sholom Aleichem wrote twelve of the *Ayznban-geshikhtes (Railway Stories)* as well as new stories of Tevye, Menakhem-Mendl, and Mottel, and the theatrical novel *Blondzhende Shtern (Wandering Stars)*. In 1913 doctors pronounced him cured of the condition in the lungs even while he contracted a painful prostate condition. Nonetheless he reentered the active world of Zionist conventions and reading tours. In the spring of 1914 he returned to Russia for what was a most successful reading tour. In addition to ovations and flowers he was approached with good offers from newspapers and even from filmmakers. In the last years of his life Sholom Aleichem developed an interest in the new art which he also satirized in his play *Dos Groyse Gevins (The Big Winning,* 1915). In the play a poor tailor loses his magnificent lottery winnings to a pair of bogus moviemakers.

Offers made in Russia in the spring of 1914 led nowhere. When the First World War began in August the whole family was gathered at Albeck, Germany. All Russian nationals were forced to evacuate the country. The family was separated and left Albeck in small groups. One daughter and her husband returned to Russia; the others went to Copenhagen, where the eldest son, Misha, stricken like his father with tuberculosis, was obliged to stay under the care of another sister. Sholom Aleichem was depressed by the coming of war, by the division of his family, and by the turn of his personal career. All Yiddish publication ceased in Russia. Only America remained. Those who could travel sailed from Copenhagen in November.

New York roused amusing satire from Sholom Aleichem, but it never pleased him. The vulgarity of the theater and the feuds of the newspapers made him uncomfortable. So did the rush of the traffic and the bravado of businessmen. Once again he made only a marginal living. At first *Der Tog* was able to give him one hundred dollars a week for two pieces; in the second year he wrote two pieces a week for *Varheit* for forty dollars. Poor health, uncertain income, and anxiety for Misha made his last two years in New York difficult. He anticipated release from a second winter in the city by a trip to California with his ailing son, but in September news came from Copenhagen that Misha had died. Sholom Aleichem lived through the winter and died in his apartment on Kelly Street in the Bronx on May 13, 1916.

Peretz and Linetski had died the year before; Mendele would die a year later. When Peretz died in Warsaw Sholom Aleichem wrote an essay in which he described their last meeting the previous spring. They met during the Passover holiday and walked about Warsaw and through its parks together with Jacob Dinesohn. They talked with great gusto about the future of Yiddish literature. Peretz, always a collector of disciples, spoke of the young writers. In the past Peretz' *tishen* ("tables") for young writers had been a feature of the literary community of Warsaw that Sholom Aleichem had not found congenial. When he was once asked if he would like to establish a "school," he answered sharply, "No, I am not *a guter Yid*"—not a good Jew, that is, a pious Jew with a following of disciples.[16] In spite of his suspicion of literary cliques Sholom Aleichem received the young writers at his apartment in the Bronx, many of them graduates of Peretz' *tishen*. Peretz Hirshbein, Sholom Asch, David Pinsky, Joseph Opatoshu, and Abraham Reisen came to him. At fifty-five Sholom Aleichem had advanced to the status of a revered "grandfather," and the new Yiddish folkwriter was a *fait accompli*, his donation to the next generation.

CHAPTER 2

Portraits of the Artist

D URING the ascendancy of the *haskalah* the primary critique of Jewish life was aimed at traditional education. The *maskilim* reassessed the *kheder* and the *yeshiva,* the primary and advanced schools, and this reassessment became the basis of much social criticism and satire. Life and learning, they claimed, were too narrowly defined in the Jewish schools. The Hebrew language was taught inadequately, and the texts studied were too few and too narrowly interpreted. Modern Hebrew writing as well as other modern studies were ignored to the detriment of Jewish youth, according to this critique. In his extremely popular autobiography, *Hattot He'urim (The Sins of My Youth,* 1876), M. L. Lilienblum blames "the bad education I had received" for his susceptibility to the cold comfort of the *haskalah.* By 1876 Lilienblum recognized that the traditional education was inadequate but that the enlightenment offered insufficient support in its place. After the pogroms of 1881 he was disabused of his earlier critique of Jewish life. "Now I am convinced that our misfortune is not the lack of general education but that we are aliens." He became a passionate nationalist.[1]

Lilienblum's career is not an uncommon example of the course taken by many Jewish writers between the 1860s and the 1880s. Disenchanted with what he considered the narrowness and the superstition of the traditional education, he turned to the new learning which he in turn found useless. By the late 1870s he was recommending more useful scientific and technical training for Jewish youth. Even when his attention was turned away from assimilation by the pogroms of 1881, he retained a critical position on the subject of Jewish education that owes much to the repudiated *haskalah.* This critique of the *kheder* and the *yeshiva* education and the parallel stringencies of the domestic life that prepared youth for these schools would provide the basis for many of the stories devoted to childhood by the early Yiddish writers.

The broad theme of education, domestic and scholastic, constitutes a genre, the *bildungsroman,* that is amply represented throughout Europe in the ninteenth century. *Wilhelm Meister, The Red and the Black,* and *Great Expectations* all tell the story of a youth growing up with more or less attention given to formal education. Since the genre is frequently autobiographical it tends either explicitly or implicitly to describe the specific education of an artist. In Joyce's *Portrait of the Artist as a Young Man* the entire process is described in the title. Taken together Sholom Aleichem's stories and novels about childhood can be read as both a broad, if somewhat mild, critique of Jewish education and as a portrait of the Jewish artist. This latter function becomes especially clear when the early stories are read in the light of the later autobiography in which most details lead to an explanation of his genesis as an author. Since before his time there were very few people who would have identified themselves as writers of Yiddish fiction, his description of the young artist has some of the freshness of Genesis. In effect, Sholom Aleichem was obliged to invent the character of this new creature. The potential artist would be both an initiate and a critic of Jewish life, an insider and an outsider. The earliest children's stories describe the making of such a person without identifying him as an artist. As the young artist evolves he is frequently identified as an orphan, a creature freed from both the restraints and privileges of family life, paradoxically detached from a community that he symbolically represents, that of *a faryossemt folk* ("an orphaned people"). The most sensitive of Sholom Aleichem's early portraits of the artist is the novel *Yosele Solovey,* the story of a young cantor who is eventually shunted to the edge of the very community whose most expressive voice he has been.

I *Home and* Kheder

Sholom Aleichem's stories of sensitive children constrained at home and in *kheder* represent a way of describing Jewish youth—and by extension all Jews—that had already become conventional when he began to write. Linetski's *Polish Boy* begins with a bitter renunciation of the hasidic schoolroom, and Mendele's story, "The Calf," describes the essential kinship of a *yeshiva* student and a calf that is bred for slaughter.[2]

In Mendele's story the boy, an orphan, develops a special affection for a calf, also an orphan. The boy and the calf join each other out of doors through a happy summer until the boy's mother notes that her son has "lost all [his] Jewish refinement." He is ruddy and healthy, like a peasant; the only cure for this healthy condition is the *yeshiva*. The *yeshiva* does its job. "In a short time it turned me into a 'real person,' with a genuine pallor and ludicrous mannerisms." He yearns for open country and curses the school. "How long shall the ground be our bed," he asks his fellow students silently as they sleep, "and the *yeshiva* our grave." In desperation he leaves the *yeshiva* and returns home to his calf, now grown into a cow. Beside her his own "emaciated figure" puts him in mind of his "wasted youth." The mother is of course delighted with her son whose appearance proves that he has been studying. "My face was now that of a virtuous Jewish child, pale and refined, and, God willing, it would serve me well in securing a bride." He returns to the *yeshiva*. Once back, the boy succumbs to hunger and is unable to support himself when he learns that a new calf born to his cow has been slaughtered, leaving his old friend desolate. He falls ill, is haunted by images of slaughter, and is taken off to the hospital on the day that he learns that "the cow, your calf, has died."

The parallel condition of the boy and his calf is a way for Mendele to describe the voluntary debility of the Jewish people. From the first Mendele makes it clear that "The Calf," like many of his stories, is to be read as an allegory. Of the original cow he says:

Like a true Jewish cow, she did penance for being in exile. Lacking a permanent lodging, she roamed the streets and slept wherever she could lay her head. . . . When it came to fasting, our cow was a paragon. She could fast for days without effort. She was simply not the glutton that gentile beasts are. Through sincere piety she gradually broke herself of the habit of feeding. . . .

In addition to this diaspora wandering and this willingness to sanctify starvation, the submissive beast is made the patient victim of drunks who stumble over her at night. What the story then describes is the place taken by Jewish education in the making of this pathetic character:

Only later did I perceive wherein the great virtue of the *yeshiva* lay: the paupers whom the *yeshiva* graduates are jolly paupers; its alumni—the *kheder* rabbis, the religious hangers-on, the general ne'r-do-wells—are un-concerned with worldly matters. And for Jews who must live in exile that is a saving virtue.

If this summary represents a later perception on the part of the narrator, the story is nonetheless intended to recreate the child's point of view. Broad application of the allegory depends on the child's tendency to assume that what he sees in the immediate vicin-ity is the way of the world: "I was a child, and like a child thought that the whole world was a copy of my village." For Sholom Aleichem as for Mendele, stories about children would be a way of analyzing Jewish life at large.

Sholom Aleichem's stories of childhood frequently describe the youthful truancy of children who are drawn away from the strict discipline of their religious education and the respectability of their particular family. Open nature, art, or adventure call them forth. A sense of guilt calls them back. Although much has been made over the years of the powers of the Jewish mother, in Sholom Aleichem's stories it is generally the plaint of a sickly father that plays on the conscience of the wayward son. These fathers are moribund tyrants who rouse pity and fear in their sons. If Mottel is the freest of these children it is because his father, Peyse the Can-tor, dies in the first story of the series. In "Dos Messerl" ("The Penknife"), "The Fiddle," and "Bay'm Kenig Ahasuerus" ("Visiting with King Ahasuerus") the father in league with the teacher represents the binding authority of the community. In all of these the socialization of the child is linked to the process of educa-tion, which for the boy might begin as early as the age of three. In Sholom Aleichem's tales of education culminating in the autobiog-graphy we see various instances of truancy as stations in the alter-nate education of the artist.

In "The Penknife" the narrator repeatedly describes the passage of time in his early life as the passage of various stages in his educa-tion.[3] At each stage he graduates to the possession of better and better knives. When he makes his first knife out of a goose quill he has just begun "to go to Yosl's *kheder* (he taught the youngest children)" and when he makes a second knife out of pieces of steel and wood he has advanced "to the study of the Pentateuch with commentaries." His next acquisition is "a real honest to goodness knife," bought from a friend when he "had just begun with the Talmud Teacher, Motti, the Angel of Death." Each of these knives is found and rejected by the boy's father who offers in their place nothing but slaps, reproaches, and books. The father no doubt sees in the blade a distraction from the studies of a son whom he already thinks sufficiently distracted. "You lout, you should be sitting over a book instead." At the same time the child's desire for whatever potency a knife affords is a reproach to his sickly father. "What did he have against my little knife?" the boy innocently asks. "How had the little thing sinned against him? Why was he so angry?"

Insofar as the inscrutable authority that the child is obliged to obey resides in men, it is fierce and uncongenial. "My father, I remember, was almost constantly ill, always pale and yellow, and in a perpetual rage at the world. He blazed with anger at the most trivial thing and was ready to trample me." At home the sickly father—"coughing and studying, studying and coughing"—is associated with books; at school, learning, guided by the man whom the children accurately call Motti *Malkhamoves* ("The Angel of Death") is just as unattractive. A hiatus of a year or two follows and brings with it a new man, quite unlike the others. A robust, amiable lodger moves in with the family, "a German Jew. A contractor named Herr Hertzenhertz." Hertzenhertz is entirely unlike any adult that the boy has known. For one thing, a "German Jew" is almost not a Jew. This "Jewish goy (or goyish Jew) . . . was bareheaded, beardless and without earlocks, and, sad to relate, even went about in a highly untraditional, short gaberdine." He neglects the simplest rituals and he speaks a halting, heavily Germanic Yiddish. And yet, as the boy observes, all these crimes go unpunished. "How come God permitted him to live? Why didn't he choke while eating?" Not only does he continue to live, he is treated around the house with the utmost respect.

Hertzenhertz, whose very existence as a Jew calls the boy's education into question, is also the owner of a remarkable knife. "And what a beauty! If only I had such a knife. How happy I would be. What things I would carve." In a moment the boy steals the knife, and the remainder of the story turns on his sense of guilt, his crisis, and his release. His guilt is not unmixed with pleasure. On a lovely summer night he anticipates the hour when everyone will go to bed and he will be free to uncover the knife, which he keeps buried in the courtyard. "Then I'd amuse myself and take delight in my little knife." But when he uncovers the knife he is pursued by the eye of the moon and struck with the fact of his crime. "I was a thief. . . . The Torah, the Ten Commandments, declared in capital letters: THOU SHALT NOT STEAL." His conviction of sin is increased at *kheder* where another boy is punished for stealing a few kopeks from a charity box. In a fit of guilt and fear he throws the stolen knife into the well and suffers a long delirious illness from which he recovers, to the relief of his chastened parents. The boy has the satisfaction of bringing the adult world to its knees. His mother assumes the child was almost lost as a result of parental sins and more specifically blames the sinister Motti, who is replaced by another teacher. In the end the boy feels a sudden rush of affection for his father, "still, how can one possibly kiss one's father?" He is rewarded and sent off to his new *kheder* making silent vows to be forever honest, "absolutely honest."

The story would seem to be a moral lesson for the "Jewish children" to whom it is addressed. Be honest. And so they may receive it. With renewed health, the boy leaves his house "like a newborn man. I pressed the Talmud folio close to my heart and ran eagerly to *kheder.*" The fact that this story is not nearly so grim as Mendele's "Calf" should not put the perils of Jewish youth out of mind. The child is recalled to family and Talmud; he has passed through a form of initiation comparable to the *bar mitzvah.* At the same time whatever passions are represented by the knife have been lost.

"The Fiddle" is also a story of truancy and return.[4] This time it is music that leads the boy astray. Here the autobiographical element is unveiled by the use of the name Sholom Nokhem Vevek's, a boy who is inspired by the town musician, one Naftali Bezborodka, who lives in "a small sod covered shack" just between home and *kheder.* Music is clearly a diversion from both domestic respectability and religious education. Bezborodka, whose name points to the suspicious absence of a beard, is "a Jew with a shortened coat, with clipped earlocks and a starched collar." In the language used to describe his family we sense a certain abundance, extravagance, and musical (if not material) plenitude that makes it a clear contrast with the sober, confined, studious home from which the young hero comes. Bezborodka reigns over a perpetually festive life; each of his dozen children plays a different instrument, and soon Sholom joins them for secret lessons on the fiddle.

The story is punctuated by a minor crisis before the final revelation of the boy's secret. Having been told by Bezborodka that Paganini—"also a Jew"—had sold his soul to the devil for a fiddle, Sholom sickens, and suffers a crisis of conscience, filled with terrible dreams of devils and fiddles. After his recovery he returns with new ardor to *kheder* where he is tested by a matchmaker and prepared for a respectable marriage. "When I became engaged I suddenly felt grown up—seemingly the same boy and yet not the same." *Kheder,* engagement, *bar mitzvah*—all the acceptable steps into Jewish manhood have been measured out for him. The order of the events is not uncommon. The custom of early marriage continued even after it was useful as a way of avoiding Nicholas' army. Few concessions were made to waywardness in the abbreviated childhood passed in the *shtetl*. But in this case Sholom's trials are not over.

Nokhem's tavern (for which we read his own father's inn) is frequented by a Russian, Tchetchek, who because of his military uniform is called "the colonel." In fact, he is a bandmaster, and he invites Sholom to visit him at home and listen to music. Tchetchek is the most seductive, amiable, and unconscious of temptors. His simple invitation leads his innocent victim out, beyond the borders of the town, into open country for music and complete freedom on Sabbath afternoons. Again natural inclination translates itself into a familial disaster that seems to outweigh the crime. Sholom's last excursion represents the essential experience of truancy in the stories of childhood:

Tchetchek lived far off beyond the town in a small white cottage with small windows and brightly painted shutters, surrounded by a garden full of bright, yellow sunflowers that carried themselves as proudly as lilies or roses. They bent their heads a little, swayed in the breeze and beckoned to me, "Come to us, young man, come to us. Here is space, here is freedom, here it is bright and fresh, warm and cheerful." And after the stench and heat and dust of the town, the noise and turmoil of the crowded *kheder* . . . I felt like running, leaping, yelling, singing, or like throwing myself on the ground with my face deep in the fragrant grass. But that is not for you, Jewish children. Yellow sunflowers, green grass, fresh air, the clean earth, the clear sky, these are not for you.

Sholom passes the barrier of the colonel's dog—the gentile world is largely marked off and protected by its dogs—and goes inside to listen to the fiddle. At the sound of the music his "soul soared far, far away into another world, into a paradise of pure sound." But he is retrieved from that other world by Ephraim Klotz, the town gossip, who brings home news of Sholom's truancy. His father is first angry and then sick; the engagement is called off, and the son, ashamed, renounces his sin:

Silently I swore to myself never, never to disobey my father again, never to cause him such grief, never in this world.
    No more fiddles.

The father's response at the end of "The Fiddle" certainly seems disproportionate to the crime. So does the broken engagement and the parental and the filial shame. The final vow seems unduly pious and a little pathetic. Sholom Aleichem is not describing the strength of a community that reclaims its young but rather its fragility. He describes the isolated Jewish communities of the Pale as they were being drawn into their last stages both by pressures from within and without. We find a parallel to Sholom Aleichem's youthful renegades in the experience of those young men who tried to renovate Jewish life in the small towns during the 1860s and 1870s. Lilienblum recalls the writing of his first articles on the reform of religious practice. His town could not bear the criticism:

My reward for this article was disgrace and dishonor, shame and sorrow. The town elders tried, on false charges, to have me banished to Siberia. . . . They incited street urchins against me; wherever I went, young rascals trailed me, shouting "Freethinker, unbeliever." Scurrilities about me were scribbled on the walls of the prayer houses, the kiosks, the outhouses. Every Saturday, preachers agitated the people against me.[5]

Word of his troubles traveled and soon he was called upon to serve the Jewish Community in Odessa. The city, especially the new and progressive city of Odessa, could absorb novelty and renovation in a way that the small town could not. It is no wonder that Odessa thrived as the center of the new literary community during the decline of the small towns.

Sholom Aleichem's critique of education in the *shtetl* was written under the influence of *haskalic* criticism. That influence diminished in the twentieth century when it became more and more clear that the small towns were fading out of existence, sometimes under the pressure of brutal assault. This sense of what was for him an already vanished land may have colored the writing of the autobiography and made the writer more benign in his recollections, but it is also largely true that in his own life the conflicts of the kind described in the two stories were not so harsh. His own education is proof of that.

In the autobiography Nokhem's disdain for the violin is not shared by the rich families of Pereyaslav, where the violin is as much a part of a fashionable young man's education as the study of German or French, "although no one expected any practical use to come of it." In Pereyaslav the music teacher is a learned Jew with "thick, heavy earlocks." All that he has in common with Bezborodka, the beardless one, is a big family of musicians. In the autobiography it is Sholom's desire for the fiddle and his father's refusal to buy him one that prompts the boy to steal a purse from a lodger. In the story the purse becomes a penknife, and a Litvak with a slightly aggressive name—Wolfson—becomes the fictional Hertzenhertz, a name that is all heart. Otherwise the story follows similar lines in both versions:

"Have you seen the knife around?" . . .
"Wha . . . what knife?"

"Have you seen the purse?" Father asked the children, and Sholom answered for everyone.
"What purse?"

Nonetheless in the autobiography the theft bears no relation to Sholom's Hebrew education. In fact, he goes off to do geometry problems while the rest of the household hunts the purse.[6] In the story he endows himself with a protective mother who saves him from his father's wrath, which is a reversal of what generally happens in the autobiography. Throughout the stories of childhood Sholom Aleichem transforms autobiographical detail in a way that emphasizes the separation of fathers and sons and exaggerates the isolation of the child from the community.

II *Orphans*

In the stories and in the autobiography it is the figure of the orphan who enjoys complete release from the authority of the fathers and of the community. Orphans are generally quite cheerful in Sholom Aleichem's stories though in reality the orphan (*yossem*) was a most pathetic character. He was uprooted from the most valued of institutions, the family, and one of the major tasks of communal charity was to make up for that loss. Describing a typical town, a character in a story by Peretz adds that "orphan boys have their 'eating days' at the tables of householders and study at the synagogue. Orphan girls become servants and cooks, or go elsewhere to earn their bread."[7] A child left with one parent was likely to remain at home or to be sent to relatives but would still be called an orphan; others were lodged at the *beys yessoyim* ("the house of orphans") and educated at the Talmud Toreh. The material benefit that such a community was able to provide was small, but its sympathy was plentiful. "Occasionally an orphan is able to exploit his sad situation and to gain privileges and favors because of it," according to Herzog and Zborowski.[8] The observation of the anthropologists confirms the plausibility of the old joke about the boy who kills both of his parents and then pleads for the mercy of the court because he is an orphan.

The joke implies the pathos and privilege of the orphan that govern the career of *Mottel, The Cantor's Son*. The first of these stories describes the death of Peyse the Cantor from the point of view of his son.[9] Until the very end of the story Mottel is able to convert the fact of his father's illness and his family's poverty into his own advantage. It is spring and the neighbor has a new calf. With his father bedridden the boy is left free to greet the season and play with the calf. Mottel's brother Elihu tries to slip into the role of the tyrant, but his threats go unsupported: "You'll catch it from father," he yells when he hears Mottel's song. "Nonsense," Mottel tells us in the running commentary that accompanies the events, "I'll catch nothing from father. Father is sick."

Mottel watches his mother and brother sell the last of the objects belonging to the family, and each loss pleases him more than the last. Each of these objects is invested with profound meaning which the mother and brother appreciate and which we as readers appreciate but which Mottel ignores. The father's holy books are sold;

the silver collar is ripped from his prayer shawl; the cabinet in which the dishes had been kept along with the sabbath *khallah* and the *matzah* at Passover is disposed of. Of course this means that the father will never use his books and his *tallis* again. He effectively dies with the loss of all the paraphernalia that identifies him in the community. Family pride and religious lore cluster around all of these objects, and their sale to the book dealer, the smith and the carpenter is utterly humiliating for everyone except Mottel. When the book dealer comes he is allowed to jump on top of the shelves; the carpenter and his helpers put on a splendid show trying to move the cabinet. Better yet is the loss of a sofa which leaves both boys sleeping on the floor, "like two princes. . . . It's a field, a joy, a paradise." Eventually Mottel himself is sold; that is, he is sent to live with the choirmaster, Hirsh-Ber. This is less cheerful. Now Mottel is removed from his friend, the neighbor's calf, and in general from the freedom that he has at home. When he finally does go home it is to see his dying father on Shavuoth. The boy is unable to grasp the idea of death until he learns that the neighbor has sold her calf to the butcher. The fact of the slaughtered calf, a frequent detail in Yiddish songs and stories, brings the reality of death into the life of the child. Why was the calf sold? "Why? Surely not to be killed! Was he born only to be killed? What is a calf born for and what is a man born for?"

At the moment when the child is struck with the idea of death, his father dies. The mother weeps as she will weep throughout the stories, but this time the boys remind her that it is Shavuoth, when the Commandments were received, and it is forbidden to weep on a holiday. "It's a yom tev—you mustn't weep," as the story is called. Until the very end of this first Mottel story, potential sorrow is mitigated by the child's independent and comic view of the world. It might be said that it is the very disintegration of the home and with it the ultimate diminution of parental authority that gratifies him. In the second story the father's death is both a release from strict guidance and a safeguard against punishment. When Mottel is slow to learn the mourner's *kaddish,* when he goes fishing, when he pulls the plugs from the watercarrier's barrels, he cannot be punished because, as everyone says, "he's an orphan." His father's death is an Oedipal dream come true. Now he sleeps with his mother and need not go to *kheder.* No wonder Mottel is the most cheerful of Sholom Aleichem's children. One side of the conflict that informs "The Penknife" and "The Fiddle" has been removed.

The repeated conflict of fathers and sons is resolved by the death of the elder or the submission of the younger. In one way or another peace is made, but the young hero can only partially be incorporated into the community. He has been touched by outside influences that leave him skeptical of power, dubious of superstition, and a latent critic of things as they are. He enjoys momentary or permanent release from the immediate hierarchy of the family, and this detachment will never wholly repair itself. In one sense these stories describe domestic rebellion in an age of general revolution for which the conflict of fathers and children is a frequent literary model and, no doubt, a frequent occurrence.

The child's desire for freedom represents an oblique political stance that happens to coincide with the position that Sholom Aleichem gives the artist in the community. What the child knows of freedom is the habitual lot of artists and orphans. In the story "Visiting With King Ahasuerus" the young hero fixes his imagination on a character who is both of these privileged creatures at once.[10] The story is told by a boy whose life is hemmed in by the tedium of family ritual. In this case he sits at Purin dinner in his grandfather's house, where the uncles and aunts and cousins regularly gather for holidays. At his side sits his teacher Reb Itzi, "my own personal Angel of Death," who corrects every transgression. It is into this dreary celebration that the Purim players come to perform for the rich man's family. The boy's heart goes out to all the artists:

But most of all I was jealous of Feivel the orphan who would don a red shirt and masquerade as Joseph the Righteous. . . . Although Joseph the Righteous was an orphan, a poor lad who bedded down in the smallest synagogue and thrived on catch-as-catch-can, and although I was the grandson of the wealthy Reb Meir, I would gladly have changed places with him just for the sake of that one day of Purim.

It is precisely *because* he is an orphan and poor that Feivel is free to adopt any role that he wishes. After the performance the rich boy creeps out after the actors and attaches himself to Feivel. From the quick dialogue between the two it is clear that it is as much the orphan as the artist that attracts the hero:

"Where's your father?" I asked him.
"I don't have a father."

"Then where's your mother?"

"I don't have a mother."

"Grandma? Grandpa?"

"I don't have grandparents."

"How about aunts or uncles?"

"I have no aunts or uncles."

"A brother or a sister?"

"I don't have a brother or a sister. I'm an orphan. I haven't got a soul in the world."

I quickly glanced at his face and then at the moon; both, it seemed, were of one color. I moved closer to him and, nimbly moving our legs, we both hurried after the gang of players.

Release with an orphan among actors is complete. They sing and dance and eat and drink until "suddenly the door burst open and I saw my father and my tutor, Reb Itzi. My heart sank within me." Clearly paupers and players have access to joys unknown or forbidden to the rich. The actors understand that the authority of the father and the teacher is also the authority in the community. One of them proposes a "blessing for the rich men of the town," and another responds with an elaborate curse. The boy is dragged away.

The fantasy that leads a child away from the restraint of conventional domestic life becomes a necessary phase in the making of the young artist in the autobiography. The autobiography is the genesis of the author, and every impluse that draws him out draws him closer to his eventual vocation. His early instructors are all orphans. The first of these is Shmulik *der Yossem* who lives with the rabbi. He is Sholom's closest friend, "and all because of Shmulik's stories." Shmulik is a companionable anthology, overflowing with tales of magic forests, frozen oceans, and hidden princesses. His source would seem to be nature—"They flowed out of him like water from an everlasting spring"—but in fact he calls on local folklore, rabbinic and cabalistic legend, and biblical tales. For example, local legend has it that Chmielnitsky buried the treasure that he robbed from Polish nobles and Jews somewhere on the other side of the synagogue in Voronko. Cabalistic lore could reveal this treasure to the rabbi if he wanted it—of course he does not—and, once revealed, the treasure would produce stones that need only be rubbed the right way to yield any further wish. Thus one story and one source leads to another. When Shmulik's protector the rabbi dies, Sholom is regaled with stories of the biblical fathers—Abraham, Isaac, Jacob, Joseph, Moses, Aaron—to whom the rabbi has returned.

Shmulik is given four chapters in the autobiography, and when he disappears after the rabbi's death, we are left with a reminder of his influence on the writer:

Did the writings of his friend Sholom Nokhem Vevek's, many years later when he had become Sholom Aleichem, reflect the spirit of the poor orphan with his wonderful stories? Who knows? One thing is certain—Shmulik had enriched Sholom's imagination, broadened his understanding, and to this day, deep in his heart, he treasures Shmulik's fantasies of riches and magic stones . . . although perhaps in a different guise.[11]

Sholom Aleichem associates the imagination of the writer with that of the child and among children his special muse is the orphan. From his early childhood, still in Voronko, he recalls a visit from distant relatives who brought with them "a servant girl, called Feigel, who was an orphan." "Feigele the Witch," the boys call her because she comes to them in the night and tells them strange stories: "She sat down among them, half-naked as she was, loosened her braids, and began to tell her eerie stories. They were not such stories as Shmulik told. Hers were tales of demons, of goblins and imps."[12] She punctuates her stories with tickles, pinches, and kisses, which probably do as much as the stories to fix her in the boy's memory. Weird stories, stolen kisses draw forth the artistic imagination.

Sholom Aleichem describes in the orphan the kind of natural storyteller that he himself was to become for the postwar critics. It was the author's intention to associate himself with this type, and this association of the folkwriter and the orphan has been perpetuated by other Yiddish authors for their own purposes. Why is the orphan specially qualified as a storyteller? In the case of Shmulik, stories are a way of reversing the order of things. In his stories he gives power to the powerless, as hungry, and as poor as the orphan. He is a born storyteller because he is born nothing else. Sholom is Nokhem Vevek's; Shmulik is nobody's. The orphan has no identity but what he contrives or improvises through storytelling.

The need of the orphan to fabricate his place in the world is a dominant theme in the fiction that developed around the *Bildungsroman*. If the adolescent hero did not happen to be an or-

phan, he generally acted as if he were. Julien Sorel bears no visible
relation to his loutish father and brothers; Dickens' Pip begins his
adventures in the graveyard where his parents are buried. In this
century, Gorki's autobiography begins with a description of his
dead father. The first part of *Felix Krull* ends with Felix shedding
tears over the body of his father, though it is probable that Felix,
like Gide's Lafcadio, is the son of an "uncle." What nearly all of
these orphans have in common is a detachment from the strictures
of a national or religious community. In Joyce's *Portrait of the Artist as a Young Man* this separation becomes the special pedigree of
the writer. In effect, Stephen disowns himself when he announces
his separation from fatherland, family, and religion. His equip-
ment, "silence, exile and cunning," draws him away from Ireland
into his art.

It is the peculiarity of the orphan hero of Yiddish literature that
he is simultaneously an outcast and a representative of the community. The further he is removed from the security of the family
the more he resembles the disinherited Jewish folk. An orphan
almost automatically acquires representative, symbolic status
among *a faryossemt folk*. The broad association of Jews and orphans is to be found everywhere. In Peretz' allegorical story, "The
Dead Town," where the care of orphans is described as a typical
communal function, the whole town is called "a grass widow" and
the townsmen "living orphans." The dead town has no legal status,
it exists on no map; it always "hung by a thread for it was built on
land on which the law said no Jew could live." It is the tenuousness
of the Jewish community in the diaspora that makes the orphan its
representative figure.

Although the Jewish community—seen as a family, a village, or
an entire population of Jews—can be represented as an orphan,
and although the community in general tends its own orphans, the
child without parents is still likely to find himself an outcast and the
butt of jokes in fiction. I. B. Singer's Gimpel is an orphan, and his
story includes traditional jokes told at the expense of orphans.[13]
Gimpel is suspicious of the woman he has been sent to court. He
asks if she is really a virgin. "Don't be deceitful with me, for I'm an
orphan." Four months after the marriage his wife bears a child:
" 'Do you think this is the way to use an orphan?' I said, 'You
have borne a bastard.' " This futile appeal for sympathy is clearly
an invitation to mockery, and Gimpel willingly serves the commu-

nity as a ridiculous scapegoat for many years. His final departure from Frampol is sudden. From one page to the next he is gone, and just as quickly we watch his conversion into a kind of sage whose gullibility has become wisdom. His dignity becomes patriarchal, and we associate him with Abraham and Moses and with the Jew wandering through the diaspora:

> I wandered over the land, and good people did not neglect me. After many years I became old and white. . . . Going from place to place, eating at strange tables, it often happens that I spin yarns—improbable things that could never have happened—about devils, magicians, windmills, and the like. The children run after me, calling, "Grandfather, tell us a story."

The victim of lies, the outcast and the orphan, becomes the teller of tales. Singer is describing himself, his own stories and his own exile. But for the Yiddish writer exile means that he shares the collective condition of his audience. Sholom Aleichem's characteristic artists are orphans and exiles but not in the sense that other European writers have described themselves as orphans and exiles. Sholom Aleichem's orphans reside on the margin of a community that has been obliged to conceive of itself as marginal. The outsider is an insider.

III *Portraits of the Artist*

The new Yiddish writer at the end of the nineteenth century tends to invent himself and his traditions in everything he writes. The writer is, in effect, a nameless orphan who makes for himself an ancestry and an identity. As we have seen, as an editor and critic Sholom Aleichem created a Yiddish literary past and named himself its present heir. And yet a past and an inheritance already suggest a kind of respectability that would be inappropriate to the Yiddish folk-writer. Over and over again in the stories and the novels and in the autobiography Sholom Aleichem recreates versions of the Jewish artist, popular singers and fiddlers, children with a yen for drawing pictures, traveling salesmen who think they can tell a story. What these people have in common is social instability and mobility that leaves them forever at the edge of Jewish society and therefore, under the paradox that governs life in the diaspora, at its very center. From these creatures Sholom Aleichem derives the true *folks-shtimme* ("folkvoice").

In the autobiography Sholom Aleichem describes his kinship with other orphans who were the natural storytellers of Voronko. The friends that he makes and the diversions that he seeks all lead to the making of the Yiddish writer. At one point he is caught writing on the wall with chalk. For this he is punished and then mocked at school. "Hudzchnik" they cry — Artist — and "Pisotel"—Author. Then, at the end of the chapter, he stands back from the catcalls and reminds us that he retained them, "indeed forever."[14] As a Yiddish writer it was his task to change the tenor of old insults into a new kind of dignity.

At the beginning of the chapter after he has been singled out as a writer on walls, he confesses that it was always his desire to become an author. A *writer* may write on walls; an *author* writes books. "His ideal," he says of himself, "was to become a *mekhaver, a-shrayber*—an author, a writer—and not just with chalk on walls."[15] His father and his father's friends support his ambition, he says, but always some assume that he will write in Russian, and others that he will write in Hebrew. No one considers Yiddish. Nonetheless he sees that his father and the others are made to laugh by a Yiddish text. They boy is impressed, vows again that he will be a writer, and turns to the subject of other artists, musicians, and cantors.

At the same time that he was writing the autobiography Sholom Aleichem also described the early growth of the artist in the character of Mottel, the cantor's son. Mottel, like the young Sholom, also works in chalk: "And I loved to draw ever since I was a child. At first I used to draw on white walls with coal, and got licked for it. Then I drew on doors with chalk, and got licked for that. Now I draw with pencil on paper, and get licked for that too."[16] His brother Elihu is shocked when his friend Pinney suggests that Mottel might become a painter. There is no dignity in painting. Elihu is determined to place his brother in a choir with a good cantor, like his father. Mottel's desire to draw is always accompanied by the sense that what he wants to do is wrong, somehow forbidden. Writing Yiddish and drawing pictures are like marking walls with graffiti.

If Mottel is destined for the visual arts, his brother's resistance is some indication of what he will meet in the world of the Jewish immigrants at the turn of the century. The ancient injunction against graven images had always limited the Jewish acceptance of painting and sculpture among the arts. Music and literature they knew. Musicians and writers were more easily assimilated into the culture. Irving Howe explains the difficulties faced by the young immigrants who set out to become painters:

> Emerging from a culture in which the very conception of visual art was still frail, the apprentice painters and sculptors of the immigrant milieu had to make a leap across both geography and history in order to test, perhaps fulfill, their talents. Even the least lettered immigrant Jew had some sense of the writer as a cultural figure who was supposed to merit respect; rarely did he have a similar sense of the artist.[17]

It is not clear that Mottel is destined to be a painter. What we see in him are the first steps of a vernacular artist, an artist who finds in daily life the stuff of his art. All around him he sees faces to draw and, like young Sholom in the autobiography, forms to imitate. In the very last episodes Mottel turns to the art that would catch his maker's eye at that time. The young boys adore "der groysen movie-star, Charlie Chaplin" and walk away from the theater imitating him.

The two works that fixed the attention of the author at the end of his life, a time otherwise dominated by personal sorrow and ill health, both describe the long apprenticeship of the artist. Even given more time it is unlikely that Sholom Aleichem would have allowed his two adolescents—Mottel and Sholom Nokhem Vevek's—to grow out of the stage of youthful vitality when, among other things, the native experience of the Yiddish folk writer was absorbed. If experience rather than special aptitude is what is required for the folk writer, then the way is made for any Jew to become a writer. One result of Sholom Aleichem's creation of the folk writer is the amusing myth that everyman can be a writer.

The prologue "To the Reader" of the *Railway Stories* purports to be the work of the traveling salesman who writes the stories:

> I am a traveler. Almost eleven months in the year I travel, mostly by train and mostly third class through all the Jewish towns and townlets. Where Jews are not permitted to live I have nothing to do.
> My, o my, what a person can see in his travels! Too bad I'm not a writer. That is, if you want to put it that way, why am I not a writer? What, after all, is a writer? Every man can be a writer. And especially in Yiddish. "Jargon." Big deal. You take a pen and you write.

This is just the opposite of the self-imposed dignity and elegance of the Hebrew writer of the *haskalah*. The credentials of the Yiddish folkwriter are not to be found in his special distinction but in his proximity to the common people, "third class." Nor is he an artist blessed with a special creative genius. All he needs is paper and a pencil, "and everything I see and everything I hear in my travels I put into my notebook." The result is not high art, just more "merchandise" that he can peddle to the press: "So I sat down and laid out the merchandise, threw out the 'seconds,' left only the best and finest, divided it into separate stories, story number one, number two, and so on. I gave each story a different name, as it is properly done—like a merchant." He has nothing to lose, not even his good name. Thus he deals with the critics. "I hid my business name. They'll never know my real name. Let them criticize, let them laugh, let them climb the bare walls. I hear them as Haman hears the rattle."[18]

In this introduction of 1909 we have the bare outline of Sholom Aleichem's early career—a businessman who writes under a pseudonym. Although the narrator of the *Railway Stories* makes only a brief appearance here and in the beginning of several stories, we are told enough to allow a certain kinship between the author and the *luftmensh* whom he creates in his stead.

If we allow for comic distortion, the character who is closest to Sholom Aleichem is Menakhem-Mendl. Through Menakhem-Mendl Sholom Aleichem is able to reduce his own most serious pursuits to a series of comic disasters from which the victim rises unharmed. In an early Tevye story where Menakhem-Mendl loses all of Tevye's savings in a misbegotten speculation we hear in the forgiveness of the victim the words that Sholom Aleichem surely would have liked to hear from his mother-in-law when he lost her fortune several years before: "For such a deed," Tevye says, "for what you've done to me, you deserve to be stretched out right here in the middle of Yehupetz and flogged. . . . The fires of Hell . . . the tortures of Gehenna are too good for you." But Tevye takes pity on his poor kinsman. "Come, brother, let's go get a drink."[19] Menakhem-Mendl is absorbed into the Tevye stories from the series of letters which began to fly back and forth between him and his wife, Sheyne-Sheyndl, in 1892. Like the Tevye stories, these bundles of letters reappeared regularly during the next several decades taking Mendl through a series of financial adventures. After ten years of failure on the bourse—or rather outside the

bourse—at Yehupetz (read Kiev)—Menakhem-Mendl turns to
writing. Of course Sholom Aleichem was writing continuously after
his return to Kiev in 1893, but it was not until 1903 when he himself
left the bourse for good that he allowed his fictional companion the
sudden recognition of his vocation as a writer. For Menakhem-
Mendl this is, at last, *a b'khovedeh parnoseh,* a respectable, an
honorable job. He writes with pride to Sheyne-Sheyndl: "I have a
new job, a brand-new job, a lovely and respectable job. I have
become, with luck, a writer. I write. You ask how I have become a
writer? It is ordained."[20] In this case the heavenly message took the
form of a kopek a line earned by another lodger at his boarding
house just for writing in the newspaper. One might say that it had
been the task of Sholom Aleichem for the past twenty years to
make Yiddish writing *laytishereh*—again, respectable—but it is in
the nature of folk writing that it cannot adopt respectability in ways
that would be conventionally recognized in Kasrilevke. Coming
from Menakhem-Mendl the *b'khovedeh* and *laytishereh parnosseh*
includes a parody of concepts that are appropriate to the leadership
of a stable Jewish community. When these terms of honor and
respectability are transferred from what was once the stable hierarchy of the Pale to a boarding house in Kiev they no longer apply.
As a boarder in Kiev-Yehupetz without the required rights of residence, Mendl cannot lay claim to the condition of life that the community requires before it bestows respectability. For Menakhem-
Mendl respectability refers to the regular income of ten rubles a
day, but just in case he was nursing more sublime notions of his
new job, Sheyne-Sheyndl corrects him in her next letter. Has he
nothing left, she asks, but to play the role of the *marshalik*? Thus
she returns the respectable writer into the jocular, transient entertainer who appears in town when there is to be a wedding. The
marshalik is one who leads the merrymakers, tells the jokes, occasionally composes an appropriate ditty, and moves on to another
town. Although once a respected figure, his status had fallen to
that of other itinerant entertainers—the *badkhonim*—and Purim
players by Sholom Aleichem's time. The wife continues to mock
her husband's new respectability by turning his phrase *a
shrayber—ich shrayb* into *a rayber gevoren un raybt*—that is, by
turning him first into a grater, say, of onions, and then finally into
one who "rubs" the seat of his pants on the benches of the railway
station in Yehupetz.

It is clear that we cannot take Menakhem-Mendl seriously as a Yiddish writer, but it should also be clear by now that for Sholom Aleichem the role of the Yiddish writer is best served when he is not taken too seriously. Sheyne-Sheyndl is right. He is related to the *marshalik,* a transient entertainer whose dignity is undercut at every turn. Sholom Aleichem maintains this image in a number of ways. In "New Kasrilevke" he plays himself, returning to his hometown to measure its progress and write a guide for other visitors. A series of episodes describing his adventures in new Kasrilevke (and incidentally describing the restaurants, theaters and hotels of the town) culminates in his return to his hotel where he finds three thieves at work. They question him to find out why he has so little money. His name means nothing to them; that is, they recognize it only as the traditional Jewish greeting:

What's your name?
Sholom Aleichem.
Aleichem Sholom. What's your name?

When they establish that Sholom Aleichem is actually his name they move on to his occupation which is no more comprehensible than the name:

I'm a writer.
We're asking you what you do, your occupation.

They assume that he has simply told them that he knows how to write. He repeats his claim:

I'm a writer.
So what do you write? Petitions or documents or denunciations?
I write articles and stories for Jewish children.
In other words you're a book vender, an author.
An author.

The thieves get the idea. First they identify their man as a book peddler, *a moykher sforimnik,* reminding us that the grandfather of Yiddish writers was also pleased to identify himself as Mendele Moykher Sforim, Mendele the Bookpeddler. Finally they agree on the proper term, *mekhaver,* "author." When they discover that the only possession of this author, a writer for the Yiddish newspapers, is a cheap cigarette case, they agree to leave him alone. "A poor beggar like ourselves."[21]

In part this is the complaint of the Yiddish writer, without honor among his own people. He makes the same complaint a year later (1902) in an essay called "Sholom Aleichem." The essay takes the form of a dialogue between the author and the *Yidishe Folkszeytung,* a newspaper in Warsaw. The Yiddish writer wants honor and a livelihood, *khoved* and *a parnosseh.* Honor he receives in the unknown towns of the Pale and a livelihood, "a great one, if he has time to be also a *melamed,* a storekeeper, a broker, a match-maker, or just a beggar who can go from house to house to collect money for his book."[22] A year later, in 1903, Sholom Aleichem could afford to quit his other pursuits and devote himself to writing. His own fame was assured. At the same time he made his alterego, Menakhem-Mendl, that veteran of most of the pursuits listed in the essay of 1902, into a Yiddish writer who thinks that he has found *a b'khovedeh parnosseh.* Up to a point this repeated harping on the honor and the income of the Yiddish writer is intended as a whimsical but real complaint. At the same time it reinforces the intended impression that the true Yiddish writer is one of the people, a pauper wandering in the diaspora like other Jews, equal to the poor thieves who try to rob him.

Orphans, thieves, *luftmenshen*—these indeed embody the majority of the Jews in the Pale though, like most majorities, they are shunted to the edge of the social hierarchy. If we look within the Jewish community rather than at its edge for the artist we find him embodied in the *khazn* ("cantor"). The *khazn* takes his place between the communal, religious function of the rabbi and the rather less respectable function of the traveling entertainer, closer of course to the rabbi. At the time that Sholom Aleichem was beginning to define the position of the Jewish artist in the *Yidishe Folksbiblyotek* as an editor and a critic, he described the evolution of an artist within the community as the story of a *khazn, Yosele Solovey (Yosele the Nightingale).*

Mazapevke, we learn immediately, is a town that values its cantors. And nowhere will you find "such extraordinary judges of cantorial music" as at the Cold Synagogue where Shmulik Yampoler sings with the help of his young son, Yosele. At first it would seem that Yosele suffers none of the conflicts known to Sholom Aleichem's other children. He is at once able to serve a religious function happily with the support of his father. But soon the familiar pattern forms itself. His mother dies and Shmulik, like Sholom Aleichem's own father, goes to Berdichev for a new wife.

And like Nokhem Vevek's he returns with a shrew. The very presence of the stepmother tends to estrange father and son. Like other children in Sholom Aleichem's stories Yosele seeks release in nature, out in the country, "his own private Garden of Eden" where he is free to sing and shout and make up little plays for solitary performance. The taste for art rises with the taste for nature. Early in the novel he is "driven from" this Eden by a band of peasant boys and their dogs. From this point his estrangement from his own community is associated with the advancement of his art; every gesture that would seem to draw him into the community has the effect of drawing him out. Having returned from his unfortunate excursion in nature, he sets out with repentant devotion to the synagogue so that he might sing his psalms in the appropriate place. On the way his eye is caught by the beauty of the setting sun, by the flight of birds, and, lost in happy distraction, he walks beyond the synagogue toward the church where he is drawn by the sound of music. He is especially taken with the sound of the organ, and his mind wanders to the time of the Temple in Jerusalem before the prohibition of instrumental music in religious service. The Polish priest speaks to him and ends the revery. Yosele runs down the hill back among the Jews, who assume he has been in the church. *Heyntege kinder,* sighs one, "today's children. So we have lived to see this." At home he is punished again.

Yosele is another orphan clearly marked for transit into the secular world of art, but since his particular art also has a place within the religious community his immediate ambitions enjoy a certain sanction. He wants to study with one of the great cantors. Through the intercession of the neighbor's daughter, Esther—also an orphan—he is sent to a nearby city where he impresses the cantor Mitzi who takes him in as a choirboy and student. He returns to Mazapevke a few years later as a handsome adolescent and a fully formed singer. The whole community squeezes into the Cold Synagogue to hear him. The ecstatic response of the listeners is not, properly speaking, an aesthetic response. They comprise a religious community, not an audience. Yet at the same time it is the quality of the voice that draws them out: "His voice was like that of a nightingale that melted their souls, anointed their hearts with balm. . . . Then his tones sank lower and lower to a whisper and almost died away, it was so light and so thin and so smooth. Then at once he raised his voice again and it was like several fiddles playing at once." The people respond to the musical quality of the voice, but it is the fact that this is a voice engaged in prayer that allows him to embody all the aspirations of the community:

Yosele finished with the words, "I have brought all of you deliverance," in a full proud tone. Those were not just the words of a cantor, but of a prophet who spoke in the name of the Almighty himself. He begged the Jews not to fall in their own esteem for they had a great God. . . . His voice gave forth such marvelous effects, sweet as honey, smooth as oil, high as the heavens, deep as the ocean. As from a dream of Eden the crowd came awake when he finished and he made the final prayer. . . . "Bring us in joy and gladness to our own land and settle us in our own country within our own boundaries." His voice seemed to weep as he sang and tears stood in people's eyes. Jews wept and spoke to God as his own children, his beloved children, his chosen ones.[23]

Yosele gives expression to the most profound wishes of a religious community. Prophetic injunctions, the "dream of Eden" and of the Land of Israel, the favored relation with God—all these find expression in his voice. The aesthetic quality releases the spiritual meaning. In *Yosele Solovey* this episode is the high point both for the cantor and the community he represents. The fall from this particular Eden is also a fall into art.

Yosele leaves Mazapevke to join the company of one Gedalia Bass as a traveling cantor, but once uprooted from the community he finds himself engaged in a more obviously commercial art. Whereas his father had to resort to respectable begging on holidays, Yosele and his manager can command a proper income. Travel itself tends to dislodge piety, especially travel in the company of professional singers. On all counts his *yidishkayt* slips away. Yosele adopts a predictable list of transgressions—card playing, pomade, sausages fried in butter on Yom Kippur—but for the practice of religious song the most noticeable of these is his tendency to turn prayer into performance. As much as his listeners favor a good voice, they cannot bear performance in the theatrical sense when it creeps into the synagogue: "A cantor is not an actor. Jews like to hear good singing with a little showmanship at the altar. But the cantor must not forget that he has been chosen by the community as a religious leader, an example for others and not as a showman, for a house of prayer not a theater."[24] This intrusion of theatricality is an embarrassment to religion. At various times the *badkhonim* had come under fire precisely because they made a show of religion. The traveling entertainers characteristically played word games with scripture and Talmud; they recited parodies of prayer and in general presented a comical alterego to the religious functionaries. The cantor, especially the traveling cantor, always treads a thin line between rabbinic prayer and entertainment. There is little chance that he will turn to parody, but the waving of arms and the rolling of eyes always threaten the decorum of religious ceremony. At the very least they call attention to the mortal performer and away from the spiritual point.

For Yosele the journey down is measured as a fall from the moment in the Cold Synagogue when he enjoyed perfect harmony with the religious community. That is not to say that the novel need be read as a defense of traditional religion. It is about the falling away of a young man from a community that inevitably defines itself through religious practice. Aside from allusions to Yosele's *kadush* there is no religious exhortation in the novel. Yosele's crimes are not mainly his transgressions of religious law, unless the infrequency of his letters home is seen in the light of the commandment to honor one's parents. His head has been turned from domestic fidelity first by the promise of wordly success and then by the blandishments of Perele *di Dame,* whom he meets on his travels. Perele, a beautiful, rich young widow, seduces Yosele, and he forgets his informal betrothal to Esther, his neighbor in Mazapevke. Yosele marries Perele and moves back with her to her home in Berdichev, that inevitable source of brides. At the same time Esther is virtually sold to the least attractive man in Mazapevke. Yosele, the prodigal son and lover, returns just in time to witness the forced merriment of the wedding feast. We are given a completely different impression of this communal festivity than we were of the sabbath eve in the Cold Synagogue. Yosele's fall is matched by the degeneration of the community. At the synagogue when Yosele sang men had danced. Now at the wedding we learn that Jews take their pleasures unwillingly, *mit gevald*, "by force," and the description of the forced drunkenness and dancing is disgusting. In this case the celebrants have every reason to be reluctant; Esther has been sold in the coldest way. But this introduction to the festivity also comes to us as a general statement about Jews. What follows is an artificially induced frenzy which is meant to make the reader uncomfortable. This is the scene that greets Yosele and drives him back, into the night.

In the end Yosele goes mad. In his delirium he sees himself attacked by Perele in the form of a cat. Finally Perele herself appears, and her presence confirms his madness. She finds Yosele singing in his old style, but his singing turns into shrieks and cries of a rooster. Yosele is sent to a nearby town where he is to be cured by the rabbi and where he remains. In the epilogue we see him several years later walking about town in one shoe and one overshoe, a large, yellow *tales kot'n*, a hat, a warm scarf for his throat, and a pair of dark glasses. In every house people make a place for him; he says a blessing and leaves without eating:

He seldom spoke to anyone. And even less often did he stand with his face toward the wall and start suddenly to chant. He did it so sweetly, with so much feeling and skill, that more than once people going by left all their business and stood and listened to him sing like a cantor. But it seldom happened that he finished what he was singing like a sane man. In the middle of his chanting, his warbling and trills, he would suddenly burst into wild laughter or begin to miau like a cat or bark like a dog or clap both hands like a rooster clapping his wings. Then he would crow, "ku-ka-ri-koo."[25]

Some pity him; children mock him. "But he bore these taunts quietly, never frowned even, answered nobody and walked with his head in the air, looking at everything through his dark glasses, happily, as though the whole world was his."

In this extreme and, one must say, melodramatic case the artist is a hero and a fool. He is either idolized or he is both pitied and mocked. He is a nightingale or he is a rooster. Although we are allowed to see Yosele's fall as a result of personal weakness, Sholom Aleichem also uses him as a guage by which he measures the entire community which had no place for him as an artist. Yosele's gift, like most gifts among Jews, is a mixed blessing. At one point we learn that it is his good looks that ruined him; elsewhere we are reminded of his kinship with the biblical Joseph whose name he bears. As a child he is told of the great boy cantor known as the Vilna Balabosel. This young man who is said to sing "just like a nightingale" charms the local count and, worse yet, charms the count's wife who makes every effort to seduce him. "When the Countess saw how things were going, she seized the hem of his coat, as Potiphar's wife had once tempted our ancestor, young Joseph." The boy escapes, but the angry countess sees to it that he is poisoned in a way that robs him of his voice, and he is left to wander about the world, poor and silent. Yosele, like Joseph and the Vilna Balabosel, is blessed and cursed by his beauty and by his voice. As a result we see him at the very center of his community singing as the voice of its best self and we see him shunted to the periphery, a ridiculous and pitiful outcast.

CHAPTER 3

Comedy and Poverty

L EYZER the Driver who takes Yosele away from Mazapevke
bound in a straightjacket summarizes the conditions of the life
he has seen:

You hear me, Reb Shmulik, you may think I am foolish. You know the
kind of livelihood we drivers and coachmen make. We see a world of
people, running or riding, this one here, that one there. It's like a Fair. I
swear to you, you may believe me, I have grandchildren, bless them, you
may take a grandfather's word for it. If you think it over well on all sides
you come up with what? *Az s'iz a paskudneh velt,* it's a nasty, wretched
world.[1]

Twenty years later Sholom Aleichem was to describe his autobiography as the report of a man returning *fun'm yarid,* from the fair.
Impatient youth goes to the fair, "his heart is full of hope; he does
not know yet what bargains he may make nor what his achieve-
ments may be. He flies toward it like an arrow. Don't stop him—he
has not time to dally!"[2] Now, returning from the fair, he has the
time to tell what he has seen. By the time Sholom Aleichem wrote
his autobiography he could adopt the authority of age with some
justice. As a young writer he sought that authority by association
with the "grandfather" Mendele whom he addresses at the beginning of *Stempenyu* and less directly through the "grandfather"
Leyzer whose voice he adopts at the end of *Yosele Solovey.* Leyzer
tells us that it is *a paskudneh velt* and at the beginning of the autobiography Sholom Aleichem would describe his own life as a
journey through "all the seven circles of Hell." Between these two
gloomy descriptions of life Sholom Aleichem wrote the stories that
would mark him as the most amiable humorist among the Yiddish
writers.

"Laughter is healthful. The doctors bid us laugh." This phrase, called "the profession of faith of Sholom Aleichem" by his French translators, appears at the end of "The Enchanted Tailor," a story that leads its innocent hero from poverty to madness, disease, and despair.[3] If we are to accept the prescription of laughter we must first understand its function in *a paskudneh velt*.

I *Laughter in a Wretched World*

Laughter that allows people to forget their sorrows needs no justification, but Sholom Aleichem rarely allows his readers to forget sorrow for long. His stories are filled with allusions to a life that is anything but funny. In his *History of the Jews,* Dubnow describes this period in a cheerless chapter called "Pogroms and the Absence of Civil Rights in Russia," and Dubnow says very little that we cannot infer from his friend's fiction. What is more, these allusions and inferences are not peripheral to the stories; it is on them that the humor rests. A story like "The Station at Baranovitch" cannot be said to induce forgetfulness.[4] At the beginning the narrator describes the cluster of subjects raised by a crowd of Jews settling down to a railway journey:

The war was bandied about for no more than five minutes and then the subject was the revolution. From the revolution it jumped quickly to the constitution and from there, naturally, to the pogroms, murders, persecutions, new decrees against Jews, the exile of entire Jewish communities from the villages, the scramble for America, as well as all other plagues, riots and disasters which made the news during those beautiful times: bankruptcies, expropriations, martial law, hangings, starvation, cholera, the anti-Semite Purishkevitch, Azev . . .

What is it that makes this list of disasters funny? Any one of them—cholera or a pogrom or further exile—could mean utter ruin, and any one of them would deserve careful attention and sympathy. As it is, we are not allowed to linger with any particular complaint; instead our attention is turned to the plenitude and rapidity of the talk. The speakers engage in verbal leapfrog as they "spring"—the verb *shpring-ariber*—from one subject to another. For the traveling salesman who narrates the *Railway Stories* all of these subjects are commonplace. The fact that each is a disaster is barely noticed. This does not mean that troubles had ceased to sting because they were so abundant in "those beautiful times." The narrator is not even describing the troubles. He is describing the velocity of talk among Jews on a train. Even if the list were neutralized by the removal of "bandied . . . jumped . . . naturally . . . scramble . . . beautiful" we would still laugh for the peculiar reason that lists of serious subjects that exceed three or four tend to be funny. Our attention and our sympathy is taxed beyond our capacity to respond with honest feeling. We are momentarily released from feeling into a euphoria that takes the form of laughter. History, ancient and modern, had presented Jews with a long list of disasters that require mourning. Comedy in this case represents a release from lamentation, though it often derives from the same source. Laughter itself is largely an involuntary response. One cannot choose to laugh. The disasters listed at the beginning of "The Station at Baranovitsh" could elicit sympathy if they were presented differently. Choice belongs to the artist or the teller of the tale. Sholom Aleichem's choice almost always includes the conversion of disaster into comical anecdote, but this is done in a way that does not necessarily eliminate pity. There is a point at which the morally responsive reader will stop laughing.

The most consistent disability for Jews throughout the Pale was poverty. "Among us Jews poverty has many faces and many aspects," Sholom Aleichem writes in a description of Kasrilevke.[5] A great part of his comedy derives from the ingenuity with which he compounds that abject condition. Kasrilevke itself is named for the *kasril,* a pauper "who has not allowed poverty to degrade him. He laughs at it. He is poor but cheerful." Elsewhere he describes the "pride of a pauper" in a way that calls his dignity into question:

> The pride of a pauper is nothing to sneer at. The poorer a man is, the prouder he is — prouder than some of the richest people in the world. I once knew a pauper who met another on the street.
> "How can you compare yourself to me, you idiot!" said the first. "You still have a pair of boots and a torn old overcoat, and I don't have these things even in my dreams."[6]

Here what the narrator chooses to call pride is really folly. If we laugh it is because normally we do not recognize superlative poverty as a goal for competition. In this case we also enjoy perfect detachment from the pauper. As a part of an anecdote inserted into a

story he remains nameless and faceless. Comic response is uncluttered with sympathy.

The story "An Easy Fast" depends on the same kind of joke, but
its extension over several pages and its grim conclusion allows sympathy which silences laughter.[7] Chaim Chaikin, an inhabitant of the
"new" Kasrilevke which boasts a cigarette factory, is himself un-
employed. He is supported by his daughters who work at the factory. The story begins:

> An experiment which the famous Dr. Tanner was not able to perform
> was carried through successfully by a poor little Jew in poor little
> Kasrilevke. Dr. Tanner set out to prove that a man could fast for forty
> days, and he tortured himself for twenty-eight days and almost passed
> away. All through the experiment he was fed teaspoonfuls of water, given
> pieces of ice to swallow, attendants sat by him day and night watching his
> pulse. It was a great event.
>
> While Chaim Chaikin showed that a man could fast much longer than
> forty days.

Chaim does not allow himself the luxury of water or ice, and unlike
"the famous Dr. Tanner" Chaim's "experiment" is unknown. He
is a poor man starving to death, but like the "Cabalists" in Peretz's
story he converts his starvation into a devotional fast. In one sense
Chaim is as foolish as the pauper who converts his poverty into a
source of pride (or as Kafka's "Hunger Artist" who converts a
squeamish appetite into the art of starvation), but at the same time
Sholom Aleichem makes it clear that Chaim commits himself to
folly for the sake of his family and that his "experiment" is controlled by deplorable economic necessity. Chaim refrains from
blaming the economic system; instead by virtue of a nonsensical reversal he blames "this wretched habit of eating:"

> "It's all because of this habit of eating that I am a poor man and my child-
> ren have to work and sweat and risk their very lives for a crust of bread.
> Just think, if a person only didn't have to eat, my children would all be
> home. There would be no more sweatshops. No more strikes. No factor-
> ies. No factory owners. No rich. And no poor. No fanaticism and no
> hatred. We would then have a true paradise on earth."

Many of Sholom Aleichem's paupers share Chaim Chaikin's tendency to indulge in utopian fantasy. In the short monologue "If I

Were Rothschild" an impoverished *melamed* dreams of infinite wealth.[8] First he will give his wife three rubles for the Sabbath. Soon he is building a roof for the synagogue and initiating vast philanthropies. There is no limit to his revery. A loan society and then a board of charity will oversee the "common welfare" of Jews everywhere. People require financial security. "For, take it from me, security from want is the most important thing in the world. Without it there can be no harmony anywhere." He is right, but the rightness is lost in the acceleration of the revery. Through the indiscriminate granting of international loans he will quell the greed of nations (and make a little interest on the side). With no more greed there will be no more war, "no more envy, no more hatred, no Turks, no Englishmen, no Frenchmen, no Gypsies and no Jews. The face of the earth will be changed. As it is written: 'Deliverance will come—' The Messiah will have arrived." At this point he is free to "do away with money altogether." Money, after all, is "nothing but a delusion, a made-up thing," which as long as it persists is the source of all strife, lust, temptation. But, says the dreamer, "without money how would we Jews be able to provide for the Sabbath?"

The Messianic moment arrives and somehow it is found wanting as it is in the old comic complaint attributed to Ibn Ezra: "If I sold candles the sun would never set; if I sold shrouds no one would ever die." And thus the little Jew shrugs off the fulfillment of the Messianic promise of eternal light and life. Sholom Aleichem's paupers are generally blinded to the real causes of their woe by Messianic dreaming. Even as he uses this endless revery as a source of comedy, Sholom Aleichem enlists sympathy for the squalor that makes these dreams necessary. The story of "Three Little Heads" is the most benign satire of the imagination of the poor.[9] The "three little heads" are the three children of Peyse the boxmaker. Peyse cuts and pastes cardboard all day and dreams of the "happy time when everything would be different, as Bebel said and as Karl Marx said, and as all good and wise men say." In that day he would change his name to Piotr Pereplotchik; he would be a Russian, not a Jew. "But until that lucky time" he stands at his boxes surrounded by his three children and wife, singing songs "some Jewish songs and some not a bit Jewish—many of them not a bit Jewish—happy sad songs with a sad happy tune." The wife who will not let him change his name chides him for his "outlandish songs. . . . Since you have come to the big city you are not a Jew any more.'' While the father dreams of revolution the children who can barely see the sky through one small window muse about free, open nature. Avremchik—the "chik" is a concession to his father's Russian revery—goes to *kheder* and knows from prayers that fruit grows on trees and that potatoes and garlic grow on the ground. He knows this because he has blessed the King of the Universe who creates the "fruit of the tree" and "the fruit of the earth.'' But this is only true in prayers. On their street there are no fields, no trees, no gardens. Occasionally they see a quarter of a chicken, and they assume a chicken has four legs. "The three children never had a chance to see anything alive.'' For the children the only release is through the stories of the eldest who tells them of trees and earth and America where "Jews have a better life and a happier one. Next year, or the year after, if all is well and someone sends them tickets from over there, they plan to go to America too.'' He tells them of America and he tells them of "the next world. . . . There is a Paradise—for Jews, of course.'' The vague promise that "next year" might find them in America matches the Passover wish—"Next year in Jerusalem"—and leads Avremchik into the promise of paradise. This religious note brings the story around to its pretext. It is a Shavuoth story. Shavuoth, the day that the Law was delivered to Moses, is also a harvest festival. In early summer, when the first grain is brought in, it is customary to decorate the house with cut grass. Peyse does this. Grass is, of course, bought at the market and brought into the ghetto where no grass grows. The story ends with the children playing in the grass on the floor of the one room where they will continue to live and where their father works and sings and dreams.

Sholom Aleichem inspires sympathy for the pain of poverty but at the same time he is prepared to make light of various phantoms contrived to eliminate that pain. In this line the dreams of the capitalist are as open to satire as the dreams of the communist. A Jew living in Russia during the first decade of this century would have known the most likely result of Peyse's naive expectation that he might become one with his Russian comrades. Many Jews who were drawn to the populist movement in the 1870s learned what they could expect as Jews from a popular movement during the pogroms of 1881. Russian radicals stood by, silent, and so at first did many Jewish radicals:

We were convinced that all Jews were swindlers and that we ought to stand
on the sidelines and not interfere. We belong to the Russian people. We
were nurtured on its labor, our minds sharpened on its literature. We, the
intelligentsia, are the brothers of the Russian people. Russian society, the
Russian intelligentsia is united with us. How comical we were, how child-
ishly naive. . . .[10]

Although Sholom Aleichem also sharpened his wits on Russian
literature, he remained skeptical of populist revolutionaries who,
like Peyse the boxmaker, are made to seem "comical" and "child-
ishly naive." 1881 and 1905 taught many Jews that solidarity with
their Russian brothers, revolutionary or otherwise, was unlikely.
The fact that the lion would remain a lion (or a bear) made the
lambs suspicious of Messianic promises.

Jewish Messianism, like Jewish poverty, "has many faces and aspects," not all of them political. As we shall see, in plays written
between 1905 and 1915 Sholom Aleichem devoted himself explicitly
to questions of class and national identity. For the present it is
enough that we recognize the place taken by the extraordinary promise in the imagination of his paupers. The imagination of the pauper is the field of a comedy in which poor people are seen scramb-
ling after a living, doing what they can to salvage self-respect, and
musing about the future.

II *Travel*

What the various movements of renewed national consciousness
active in Russia after 1881 have in common is the desire to instill in
the Jewish masses a strengthened sense of identity. A long history
of humiliation, poverty, and periodic physical assault threatened to
erode even the most elementary forms of self-respect for millions of
Jews while others drifted toward assimilation as a result of promises or threats. The fragile sense of individual and collective identity
became a favorite theme of the Yiddish humorists. Sholom
Aleichem's paupers are always on the verge of forgetting who they
are, but the identity is especially likely to become unhinged when
the Jew travels away from home.

In "Home for Passover" the poor *melamed,* Fishl, is obliged to
travel twice a year.[11] He works in Balta and lives in Hashtchavata.
For the High Holidays and at Passover he crosses the River Bug to
spend the holiday at home with his wife and children. The perilous

trip over the Bug during the spring floods is the occasion of this story. Fishl's trip home is described as a return from his "exile among strangers," and the allusion is enriched by the fact that he comes to the shores of this northern version of the Red Sea at Passover, the holiday that promises return from Jewish exile. In this case the promised land is home and the wilderness is the Ukrainian countryside with its wild rivers and boisterous peasants. Living in two worlds Fishl is two people. At home he is allowed to think of himself as a Hebrew prince; on the road he is an insignificant Jew. His anticipation of the first seder is regal: "His 'throne' is ready—two stools with a large pillow spread over them. Any minute now Fishl will become king, any minute he will seat himself on his royal throne in a white robe, and Bath-Sheba, his queen, with her new silk shawl will sit at his side. . . . Make way, fellow Israelites! Show your respect! Fishl the *melamed* has mounted his throne! Long live Fishl!"

When we meet him in this story Fishl is not among his fellow Israelites but caught on the wrong side of the Bug with his home, the Sabbath and the first seder all on the other side. His company is made up of two peasants, one the carter Feodor, the other the ferryman Prokop, and the comedy of the story resides in the contrast between the way he is seen by the Russians and the way he sees himself. The dual identity is expressed in the duality of language. Fishl speaks to the boatman "half in Russian, half in Hebrew, and the rest with his hands." In the turmoil of the crossing among high waters and dangerous ice floes the two languages rise in a strange duet as Fishl chants the words of Jonah—"The waters compassed me about"—while Prokop celebrates the spring floods with a Russian song—"Oh, you waterfowl." Fishl transports himself into a biblical revery while in the eyes of the Russian he is the most insignificant of little creatures:

"Why is he so afraid of death, that little man?" Prokop Baraniuk sat wondering, after he had got away from the icefloe and pulled his bottle out of his pocket again for another drink. "Look at him, a little fellow like that—poor, in tatters. . . . I wouldn't trade this old boat for him. And he's afraid to die!"

And Prokop dug his boot into Fishl's side, and Fishl trembled. Prokop began to laugh, but Fishl did not hear. He was still praying, he was saying Kaddish for his own soul, as if he were dead.

Under the pressure of fear the traveler is completely unhinged from himself. He says his own Kaddish, and a moment later when his mind turns to the biblical precedent of the Red Sea crossing, he casts himself out of the identity of the victorious Jew and into the role of the sinking Egyptian. He recalls the words of Moses' song in Exodus. "They sank as lead in the mighty waters." Only on shore, safely engaged in traditional ritual, is Fishl rehinged. He acknowledges the "miracle from heaven. We can thank the Lord. He takes care of us." The identity made fragile in its exile is reintegrated at home.

Hashtchavata is a haven for Fishl the Melamed. There he is known and respected. It is only in the outside world that he is diminished so lamentably. A more frequent figure in Sholom Aleichem's stories is the character who is hounded within the *shtetl* itself, indeed, within his very home. This unlucky outcast is doubly removed from his proper self when he is lost in transit.

In "On Account of a Hat" Sholom Shakhnah, like Fishl the Melamed, is hurrying home for Passover when he becomes unhinged.[12] But unlike Fishl, Sholom Shakhnah is marked from within his own town as a special brand of fool. We have the immediate testimony of the Kasrilevkite who tells the story to Sholom Aleichem. Both teller and listener in this case are also heading home for Passover and the story places them in the position of its eventual subject, Sholom Shakhnah, who is identified as "Sholom Shakhnah Rattlebrain . . . absentminded . . . a distracted creature." The Kasrilevkite merchant continues his introduction. There are many stories told about this scatterbrain, he says—"bushels and buckets of stories—I tell you, whole crates full of stories and anecdotes." In effect, he prepares Sholom Aleichem for a familiar kind of story told about a familiar kind of person, the fool. He protests that this story is true and Sholom Aleichem chimes in to reinforce his point before the tale begins, but we have been prepared to enter a convention of "stories and anecdotes" of a kind that are told to pass time among travelers. Within the genre it is to be a story of a person branded by his own community as a fool; in this case the fool is also a traveler.

Sholom Shakhnah enters the station at Zlodievke where his only chance for rest after two sleepless nights is to sit next to a magnificently uniformed Russian official. Before he sleeps he pays the porter Yeremei to awaken him in time to catch the last train that would get him home in time for Passover. For the benefit of the "goyisher kop" Yeremei, Sholom Shakhnah describes Passover as "our Easter." Sholom Shakhnah, we are told, has "a Yidisher kop," a Jewish head. Now under certain circumstances it may be praiseworthy to have a truly Jewish head. In this case "a yidisher kop" means that Jewish wisdom has gone astray in a particularly Jewish way. According to numberless tales the town of Chelm is full of such wisdom:

Someone saw a Chelmite writing a letter in an unusually large hand and asked, "Why such huge letters?"

"I am writing to my uncle, who is—may you be spared the like—very deaf."[13]

We are prepared for more in this line by the preliminary stage of the story.

Having hired Yeremei as his alarm, Sholom Shakhnah falls asleep beside the Russian official on the bench. He sleeps "with his head thrown back and his hat rolling away on the floor." The fall of the hat reveals the complete loss of control on the part of the Jew. The detail of the fallen hat is used similarly by Joseph Conrad to indicate the death of Verloc in *The Secret Agent.* Verloc habitually wears his hat and overcoat indoors. When his wife stabs him as he lies reclining on the sofa we know the consequence indirectly through the fall of his hat which then remains the focus of the scene. For the Jew in Sholom Aleichem's comic tale the loss of the hat represents a moment of especially unguarded carelessness, for a Jew is enjoined to wear a hat at all times. At night a *yarmelkeh* is kept within easy reach. Without the hat an essential element of his Jewish identity is missing. In this case the whole turmoil of travel and the loss of the hat enter Sholom Shakhnah's dreams as he sleeps. In a dream he is riding home for Passover in a cart driven at a snail's pace by Ivan, a local peasant. Sholom Shakhnah explains his needs as he has explained them to Yeremei. Speed is necessary, and Ivan begins to make such haste that Sholom loses his hat: "He covered his head with his hands. . . . How can he drive into town bareheaded?" Of course he would be ashamed to be seen without a hat and, in addition, without a hat he has lost his identity. Suddenly Yeremei awakens him. Sholom Shakhnah, lost in the middle land between sleep and waking, confuses Yeremei for Ivan. What both dream and reality have in common is that both have left him hatless. He is aware of this and as a reflex action he grabs what turns out to be the official's hat with its impressive red band and visor. Everyone in the station responds to a change of identity of which he is unaware. He walks to the ticket window and the crowd makes way. The ticket agent addresses him as "Your Excellency." On the platform an obsequious conductor leads him out of a third- and into a first-class carriage. Sholom Shakhnah is completely perplexed:

[He] rubs his forehead, and while passing down the corridor glances into the mirror on the wall. It nearly knocks him over! He sees not himself but the official with the red band. That's who it is! "All my bad dreams on Yeremei's head and on his hands and feet, that lug! Twenty times I tell him to wake me and I even give him a tip, and what does he do, that dumb ox, may he catch cholera in his face, but wake the official instead! And me he leaves asleep on the bench! Tough luck, Sholom Shakhnah old boy, but this year you'll spend Passover in Zlodievke, not at home."

He runs back into the station to wake himself up and, of course, misses the train back to Kasrilevke.

In Sholom Shakhnah's pseudological jump we have the *yidisher kop* run amuck, and the result is a joke on the Jewish mentality told in the spirit of the tales of Chelm. But the specific form taken by this bit of illogic in Sholom Aleichem's story represents more than a comic flaw of reason. In the moment that he is posed before the mirror, Sholom Shakhnah sees another person, an antithetical self so radically detached from probability that even he, a fool, does not believe it. His disbelief is so potent that it splits his personality and leaves the more substantial half intact on the bench. He returns not simply to retrieve his hat but to retrieve himself.

Sholom Shakhnah's confusion begins before he looks in the mirror. He is perplexed by the unwonted deference of the crowd, the ticket agent, and the conductor. We can assume that no one has ever made way for Sholom Shakhnah, no hat has ever been tipped to him, no politeness rendered. His habitual identity has been fixed by the response that he generally arouses, and that, presumably, is utter neglect or mockery. The gentile world knows him only as a Jew; the Jewish world knows him as a fool. The erosion of his identity completes itself when he is treated with deference. He sees himself treated in a way that is generally reserved for people of power, wealth, and official status, rarely for Jews and never for him. At this point most people would turn around to see if this unfamiliar treatment was being aimed at somebody else. He cannot even make an impression on a mirror. In this extreme case of the kind of invisibility described by Ralph Ellison in *The Invisible Man,* the Russian Jew loses sight of himself. He has adopted the tendency of his society to identify people by external signs. In this case the change of costume effects the vast transformation of a Jew into a gentile, a change that is enlarged by the original lowliness of the Jew and the official status of the gentile. Sholom Shakhnah's acceptance of his social and superficial identity makes the simplest recognition of an internal continuous self impossible.

Y. L. Peretz concludes his argument against the willing concessions made by assimilated Jews with a similar example. These people voluntarily disperse themselves in accord with the needs of the gentile community: "If two of you found yourself in the same place, one got away from the other. Two in one spot at one time might be more than the others would welcome. If one of you happened to look into a mirror and to see his own face there, he jumped aside, he did not recognize his own mask, he thought there was another person in his way.[14] The position of the assimilated Jew is quite different from that of Sholom Shakhnah, but the results are similar. "On Account of a Hat" pretends to be the bizarre tale of an eccentric fool, but it is the story of a Jew whose madness is a comic exaggeration of a representative malady—the utter annihilation of the self that might follow centuries of isolation and denigration in a larger, dominant community.

Within the community we might expect the Jewish *shtetl* to be a refuge for a man like Sholom Shakhnah. His nightmare in the station indicates the urgency of return and his compulsion to avoid the gentile world, especially at Passover time. The *melamed* in "Home for Passover" at least enjoys domestic compensation for his diminution in the outside world, whereas Sholom Shakhnah is mocked by his wife and taunted by the community of Kasrilevke. The people of the town, especially the children, make him a laughingstock. They tease him about his momentary excursion into officialdom and refuse to believe him when he says that he was delayed by business. He accuses them of making up the story. But, asks the Kasrilevkite narrator in conclusion, "you think it's so easy to put one over on Kasrilevke?"

It is not really important how we answer the final question. In spite of the protestations of both Sholom Aleichem and the narrator at the beginning of the story, we know the entirety to be a fiction. At best we are to believe that this is the kind of story that one traveler tells another as they travel home for Passover. But in another sense the story of the red cap and the mirror *is* true. It is not the truth of verisimilitude but rather it is the truth of accurate legend. What seems to be fantasy is made less fantastic by what Sholom Aleichem's original readers would have known and by what we may infer of social conditions within the Pale. Under these conditions the identity of a poor Jew might be annihilated, and however fantastic the form of that annihilation we are ready to receive it as we receive the myths and fables of the Greeks, as pre-scientific folk renditions of the truth. The justification of his own use of fable that Peretz inserts in his autobiography helps to explain a mode that is no less common in the writing of Sholom Aleichem:

The fable is also a truth, and may reveal more reality than the mere facts. Man conceals his will and hides his true identity; in his actions, he is governed by convenience and propriety. But people understand the hidden essence of Man, and the fable they construct about him narrates what he would do, if he were true to his own self. In the fable, what actually has happened to him, if not for accidental interventions, would emerge in vivid colors.[15]

In the story of the hat, the "true identity" that is revealed through the vehicle of fantasy is, in effect, the absence of identity which Sholom Aleichem sets out to describe in his comic rendition of life in the Pale.

Another travel story, "Two Anti-Semites," describes the incomplete demolition of the Jewish identity.[16] Max Berlyant is a traveling salesman whose business takes him places where it would be best if he were not known to be Jewish. But, unfortunately, he is neither invisible nor inaudible. He is blessed with an undeniably Jewish nose and with an unmistakable accent. Since he is obliged to travel and talk, "he had to be seen *and* heard." In order to counteract the nose and voice, he shaves his beard and indulges in non-kosher food at every railway buffet. Now he finds himself traveling through Bessarabia shortly after the Kishinev pogrom. The pogrom brought him great pain, and he wants neither more news of it from Jews nor insults from Gentiles. In a station along the way he decides to buy a copy of the *Bessarabian,* a newspaper edited by P. A. Krushevan, the infamous anti-Semite who had effectively started the pogrom at Kishinev with false reports of a ritual murder. The narrator tells us that this paper disgusts Jew and Gentile alike. Once back in his compartment Max covers himself with the newspaper and goes to sleep certain that no one, certainly no Jew, will invade his privacy. But by chance the next person to enter is another semirussified Jew named Peti Nyemtchik, who, in spite of his name, "liked his own people and adored telling stories and anecdotes about them." Max's newspaper has slipped, revealing the nose, and Peti senses the possibility of an anecdote that he cannot resist. He buys his own *Bessarabian* and stretches out on the opposite bench. Meanwhile Max suffers from terrible dreams of pigs and lobsters, the wailing of "Ki-shi-nev" and the grotesque replacement of his nose by a copy of the *Bessarabian*. When he wakes and sees someone sleeping under the same newspaper, he is dumfounded: "He imagined that it was he himself he saw stretched out on the other bench. Max could not understand what in the world he was doing on the other bench, and how anyone could possibly see his own reflection without a mirror. Max felt his hairs bristling, standing up one by one." He comes to his senses and the "two Bessarabians" regard each other with curiosity. Suddenly inspired, Peti begins to whistle the familiar song "Oif'n Pripetchik." Max whistles the next line and together they conclude the refrain. The "well-known Yiddish song" that they sing had been written not long before by Sholom Aleichem's friend M. M. Varshavski, whose songs took their place in the conscious folk revival of those years. In this story we see the minor awakening of a slumbering consciousness after the most recent round of pogroms. Max Berlyant's identity, in this case a specifically Jewish identity, is shaken by the exigencies of travel, and then it is renewed. The nose in this story is less removable than the hat in the other story and can only be lost in a Gogolesque nightmare. As in the story of the hat, the dreamer awakes to see a perplexing alterego that in this case brings with it a certain enlightenment.

In both stories comedy originates in the very conditions that rendered Jewish life in czarist Russia humiliating and dangerous. Stories that are based on the political alienation of the Jew induce the kind of spiritual and psychological alienation that has become a byword in modern literature. The assault on the identity undergone in travel recommends the observation of the grandfather in Kafka's "The Next Village":

My grandfather used to say: "Life is astoundingly short. To me, looking back over it, life seems so foreshortened that I scarcely understand, for instance, how a young man can decide to ride over to the next village without being afraid that—not to mention accidents—even the span of a normal happy life may fall far short of the time needed for such a journey."[17]

Sholom Aleichem primarily concentrates on the "accidents," but like Kafka he also suggests in his darkest comedies that human existence is itself a perilous venture.

III   *The Limits of Laughter*

We read Sholom Aleichem's comedy with full knowledge of the general precariousness of life in the Russian Pale. Even as we laugh we are not allowed to forget for long that the source of our laughter is also the source of lamentable pain. This is perhaps best exemplified in the story that ends with the familiar injunction to laugh. It is when Shimmen-Eli, "The Enchanted Tailor," has gone mad and is about to die that we are told that "laughter is healthful. The doctors bid us laugh."[18]

Shimmen-Eli is instructed by his wife, Tsippa-Beyla-Reyza, to take his few rubles to the next town and buy a goat from the wife of the local *melamed.* His family wants milk and cheese. Going and coming from his errand he stops at the tavern of his kinsman, Dodi Rendar, who gives him a drink each time and exchanges the she-goat for a he-goat behind the scenes. The goat that produced buckets of milk for the *melamed's* wife is dry for Shimmen-Eli's wife. And when the tailor tries to return the animal he can never prove his point because Dodi repeats the exchange. Shimmen-Eli, rebuked, mocked, and thoroughly perplexed, goes mad. During the day he is ridiculed by children; at night he chases his mysterious goat through the town. He is haunted by the dead who pray in their shrouds at the old synagogue and by a bird shrieking from the church steeple. Dead friends appear to him along with ghouls and vampires and strange creatures that move about on tiny wheels. We leave him struggling with the "Angel of Death." Shimmen-Eli's ultimate sorrow (*troyer*) would seem to preclude comedy. But that is not the case. In fact his sorrow and his comedy derive from the same condition. Shimmen-Eli is a *nebekh,* a poor, unfortunate creature who is at the same time a source of comedy, the inevitable butt of jokes. The *nebekh,* in this case, is a pompous fool but he is also a victim of social conditions which he shares with most other Jews in the Pale. His folly and his pomposity are funny; his poverty is not. But since the two go together it is not always clear where the humor of one ends and the pathos of the other begins.

Shimmen-Eli is called "Shma-koleynu"—Hear our voice [O Lord]—for the loudness of his voice in prayer. He constantly parades his vast knowledge of holy texts in a way that indicates that it is not vast. For scriptural accuracy he competes with Tevye. At the same time he lords it over his cousin Dodi, showering him with citations and mocking him for his ignorance in a way that almost justifies Dodi's revenge. Shimmen-Eli's pedantry is matched by his childlike simplicity, and it is as a child that we see him set forth into the countryside on his way to buy the goat. The description that follows sounds remarkably like the descriptions of the countryside into which children in other stories are released from home and *kheder:*

> It was Sunday, a bright, warm, summer day. Shimmen-Eli could not remember when he had seen a beautiful day like this before. He could not remember the last time he had been out in the open country. It had been a long time since his eyes had beheld such a fresh green forest, such a rich green carpet sprinkled with many-colored flowers. It had been a long time since his ears had heard the twitter of birds and the fluttering of small wings, such a long time since he had smelled the odors of the fresh countryside.

It is not strict parents or a long winter that keep the adult from open country; it is poverty.

> Shimmen-Eli Shma-Koleynu had spent his life in a different world from that. His eyes had beheld entirely different scenes: a dark cellar with an oven near the door, with pokers and shovels leaning against it, and nearby a slop-basin full to the brim. Near the oven and the basin, a bed made of three boards, with a litter of small children on it, half-naked, barefoot, unwashed, always hungry.
>
> His ears had heard entirely different sounds: "Mother, I want some bread! Mother, I'm hungry!"

At this point Shimmen-Eli's political sympathies translate themselves into a brief and humble utopian fantasy: "What harm would it do if every workingman could come out here at least once a week, here in the open country, and enjoy the freedom of God's great world? Ah, what a world, what a world.''

Shimmen-Eli's yearnings may reflect the humanitarian impulse almost axiomatic in Yiddish fiction of the period, but the way he expresses his sympathies is open to satire. He rants against the powers of the town, the tax-collectors, the rabbis, the ritual butchers, and the philanthropists all in the vein of Mendele's early satires, *Dos Kleine Menshele* (1863) and *Di Takse* (1869), and of Sholom Aleichem's *Elections,* which all adopt Shimmen-Eli's stance against the powers of the community who enrich themselves at the expense of the poor. The crimes remain to be chastened but those who chasten cannot be ignored by the satirist. When Shimmen-Eli indulges in drink he tends to rant:

May the devil take them, those givers of charity! Is it their own money they give? All they do is suck the blood of us poor people. Out of my three rubles a week they make me pay twenty-five kopeks! But their time will come, never fear. God shall hold them to account. Although to tell you the truth, my cherished wife . . . has long told me that I am worse than a shlimazl, a fool and a coward, because if I only wanted to use it, I could hold a strong whip over them!

Here as in "Three Little Heads" Sholom Aleichem makes fun of the naive, henpecked revolutionary, but it is just this naiveté which is used elsewhere to make his condition especially pathetic.

Shimmen-Eli goes back and forth and between the two towns with his goat. He enlists his fellow tailors to represent him against the thieves of Kozodoievka, the town of goats. But nothing can solve the problem of the goat's dual identity. In the end Shimmen-Eli goes mad and is last seen "struggling with the Angel of Death." The child crying beside his sickbed, "Mama, I'm hungry," reminds us that this is the story of people who are miserably poor. Shimmen-Eli is sick, and unlike the preadolescent fevers and nightmares suffered in the stories of children, this one does not promise to end in health and growth into sadder but wiser adulthood. It is with this grim knowledge of inevitable decline that Sholom Aleichem leaves his hero and shifts his emphasis at the end of the story:

The end was not a happy one. The story began cheerfully enough, but it ended like most cheerful stories, very tragically. And since you know that I am not a gloomy soul who prefers tears to laughter and likes to point a moral and teach a lesson, let us part as cheerfully as we can. And I wish that all of you readers and everybody else in the world may have more opportunities to laugh than to cry.

Laughter is healthful. The doctors bid us laugh.

The coda may be used to identify Sholom Aleichem as a master of laughter, but it is questionable whether this story allows his conversion into a comical medicine man. At this point "The Enchanted Tailor" has ceased to be funny. To laugh at the bedeviled tailor would be brutal. When the frequently isolated phrase is returned to its context, we can only conclude that Sholom Aleichem does not mean what he says. A healthy laugh would indicate a failure of sympathy that the author does not mean to encourage. Nor are we to accept his disclaimer of moral interest.

If the act of reading can be said to engage our moral selves, laughter may not always be an appropriate response. The task, then, of writers who have both moral and comic pretensions — Swift, Dickens, Sholom Aleichem — is to teach us when laughter must stop. Toward the end of Swift's "Modest Proposal" a reader with an active sense of irony must stop smiling and begin to take notice of the deadly seriousness of the essay. The writer proposes that Irish babies be sold as a delicacy to the English, who in any case are sure to get them sooner or later. A less sensitive reader who does not "get" the joke at all may have remained sober throughout and will therefore not register the intentionally serious turn of the essay when it comes. The dedicated satirist cannot afford to leave his readers laughing throughout. Too many readers will assume that laughter is benign—"healthful"—and tend to disregard its lessons. A morally responsive reader cannot put Swift down with a smile.

"The Enchanted Tailor" includes an explicit correction of laughter. "What are you laughing at?" a workingman cries at the town gossips. "You ought to be ashamed of yourselves! Grown men with beards. Married men with families. Shame on you! Making fun of a poor tailor. Can't you see the man is not himself?" The doctor, when he comes, is a useless fool, and sympathy at this point comes too late:

Wonder of wonders! For fifty years Shimmen-Eli Shma-Koleynu had lived in Zolodievke in poverty and oppression. For fifty years he had lain in obscurity. No one spoke of him, no one knew what sort of man he was. But now that he was so close to death, the town suddenly became aware of all his virtues. It suddenly became known that he had been a good and kind man, generous and charitable; that is to say, he had forced money out of the rich and divided it among the poor.

The voice of the satirist interrupts the narration in order to identify the deplorable conditions that yield creatures like Chaim Chaikin, Sholom Shakhnah and Shimmen-Eli.

IV   *The Tevye Stories*

We have described the comical victim in Sholom Aleichem's stories as a Messianic dreamer. It is not only the utopian dream but the daily life of the Jew that is rendered comical by the contrast between the fact of the diaspora and the distant prospect of Messianic redemption. What Gershom Sholem describes as "the price demanded by Messianism" is also the source of much that passes for humor among Jews. "Jewish Messianism is in its origins and by its nature . . . a theory of catastrophe"[19] and so is Jewish humor. It is no accident that both share a yearning for a utopian age which will call a halt to the catastrophic conditions upon which both depend. Comedy that describes conditions as they get worse and worse would be unbearable if it did not derive from a religious disposition that anticipates the arrival of the Messiah in the worst of times. Messianic thinking, with its peculiar blend of pessimism and hope, is the spiritual base for most of Sholom Aleichem's comic monologues. The most sustained example of hope that survives disaster and even seems to derive from it is the series of stories devoted to *Tevye der milkhiger.*

The eight Tevye stories appeared separately between 1895 and 1914.[20] In each successive story Sholom Aleichem seems to try to invent a worse situation for Tevye, and the stories taken together can be seen as a more and more severe test of his original principle, stated at the beginning of the first story: "So long as a Jew can still draw breath and feel the blood beating in his veins, he must never lose hope." In the first story hope is justified. Tevye receives thirty-seven rubles and a tired milch cow for helping two rich women out of the woods near the summer resort at Boyberik near Yehupetz. With the money and the cow he establishes himself as *a milkhiger,* a milky as opposed to a meaty person, that is, a dairyman who delivers his produce throughout the neighborhood but especially in Boyberik. In the next story, "The Bubble Bursts," his trials begin. He invests all his savings in the speculations of his kinsman, Menakhem-Mendl, and of course he loses everything. The next five stories describe the fate of five of his seven daughters. In varying degrees each daughter contributes to her father's sorrow. In "Modern Children" the first rejects an arranged match and marries by choice an impoverished tailor. The second daughter, Hodel, also defies the conventional use of the matchmaker and marries a young revolutionary whom she follows into exile. Even in her absence she remains Tevye's favorite, and he uses her strength as an example for a younger, weaker sister. The first two daughters reverse certain conventions, but they leave the structure of the family and the religion intact. The third daughter, Chava, commits the unforgiveable crime. She converts and marries a Christian. This may be the worst in the series of disasters that follow. In his book on the Yiddish language Maurice Samuel describes *shmad*—"conversion"—as "the heaviest and deadliest Yiddish word," and the word *meshumid* —"the convert"—carries with it an historical sense of profound betrayal. The apostate often became "the assistant, or even the renewed inspiration" of the oppressors. In a rigorously divided society the convert, having stepped into the enemy camp, was mourned as dead.[21]

Tevye's next daughter, Schprintze ("Hope"), commits suicide when she is abandoned by a rich young man whose family does not approve an alliance with the daughter of a dairyman. Tevye is made to grieve both for the death and for the humiliation. In the next story, "Tevye Goes to Palestine," his daughter Beilke acts in a way that would seem to answer her father's dreams. She accepts an arranged marriage with a rich man. But curses may be blessings and blessings often bring with them a curse. Beilke's husband, the war profiteer Padhatzur, is as rich as the family that rejected Schprintze, and like them he is also ashamed of his connection with Tevye. Aside from the czar and his officials, these bearers of new wealth are the only villains in the Tevye stories. Padhatzur encourages Tevye to get out of sight, to leave the country. Beilke is sad and silent. "Hodel would have done otherwise," her father tells her:

"Don't compare me to Hodel," she said. "Hodel grew up in a time when the world rocked on its foundations, when it was ready at any moment to turn upside down. In those days people were concerned about the world and forgot about themselves. Now that the world is back to where it was, people think about themselves and forget about the world.''

Of course, she is deluded in thinking that the world will allow itself to be forgotten long. The official reaction after the revolution of 1905 had begun as a return to normal and had reached its nadir by the time of the late Tevye stories (between 1909 and 1914). Renewed nationalism not only rendered the liberalizing manifesto of October, 1905, useless but added new restraints on Jews. As a living symbol of the reaction, a Jew, Mendel Beilis, remained in prison in Kiev from March, 1911, to October, 1913, when a Russian court was unable to convict him of ritual murder. In the last Tevye story, "Get Thee Out," Tevye is obliged by czarist decree to remove himself from his rural home as part of the policy that had been squeezing Jews out of the countryside and into towns. Tevye, one of the few to remain in a rural village, is last seen taking another step in the Jewish exile.

The headnote to the first story prepares us for the milieu of poverty with the praise of God: "Who raiseth up the poor out of the dust, And lifteth up the needy out of the dunghill" (Psalm 113). These lines which can be taken as a promise of spiritual redemption can also be taken to mean national renewal, socialist revolution, or simple economic endowment, which is what it means in this particular story. Those who know the Psalm—and that would have included most of Sholom Aleichem's readers— would know the lines that follow:

> Giving them a place among princes,
> Among the princes of his people;
> Who makes the woman in a childless house
> A happy mother of children.

Sholom Aleichem often describes the amusing and unlikely expectation of the Jewish pauper that he will graduate without delay to instant princedom. What is far more likely is that his wife will be "a happy mother of children." Those who recognize the two lines of the headnote from Hannah's prayer of gratitude after the birth of Samuel (I Sam. 2:1-10) recall that "the barren woman has seven children." Tevye's Golde has seven, all daughters. Families in the Pale were large—seven would not be unusual—but seven daughters may be too much of a good thing. The blessing of children is not exactly transmuted into a curse, but it is made to represent a comic distortion and a certain reversal of parental expectations.

All daughters means no sons, and it is primarily the son who brings honor to his parents through religious scholarship and who prays for them when they die:

A girl is also a blessing, and receives the affection and care showered on all children. She too may make a marriage that will enhance the family *yikhus* [honor, status], but in order to do so she must have a dowry and marrying off daughters is likely to be a serious problem. Therefore they say, "Many daughters, many troubles, many sons, many honors" and "If you have daughters you have no use for laughter."[22]

To which Tevye adds, "Brodsky has money, I have daughters."

Tevye's daughters are, as the title of one of the stories suggests, *heyntege kinder* (today's children, "Modern Children"), and the choice of daughters and not sons as the most modern of children cannot be overlooked. It appears that in a society traditionally governed by men for religious reasons, women enjoyed readier access to local and secular languages and might more readily answer the invitation to read and write and think and act in a world generally closed to them. It was likely to be in a modern way that young women would satisfy their intellectual curiosity while their brothers were bound to those "Angels of Death," the teachers of Hebrew. As we have seen, the stories that Sholom Aleichem wrote about children were about generally rebellious though ultimately acquiescent boys. In the Tevye stories the perennial conflict of fathers and sons gives way to the complex relation of a father and his daughters. The initially comic twist of a man blessed with seven daughters is given a further serious twist by the fact that it is precisely daughters who at every point will test and question the traditions their father lives by.

Tevye's daughters can read. "Yiddish and Russian both," he says of Hodel. "And books—she swallows like dumplings." Although Tevye is proud of this literacy it also draws his daughters away from him. Hodel's revolutionary, Feferel, is also her teacher, and when Tevye first sees Chava and the Russian clerk, Fyedka, together they are exchanging Russian novels. Chava, like Sholom Aleichem, is an avid reader of Gorki, but in the story this attachment is associated with her fall. Similarly in another story, "A Daughter's Grave" (not in the Tevye series), another modern girl, "a high school graduate," reads along with the cantor's daughter a forbidden book, "*Sani* by Archie Bashes," as her father says. The book is the popular *Sanine* by Mikhail Artzybasheff (1907), and it includes a suicide pact that sets a sinister example for the two girls.[23] In a lighter vein Sholom Aleichem is fond of describing another kind of modern young woman, the "mademoiselle" like "the charming young lady who finished four terms of high school, read Artzybasheff, spoke Russian and not a word of Yiddish, mind you, and never so much as lifted a finger" and usually pounds the piano and chirps French.[24]

In the Tevye stories we are to understand that it is books and discussions outside the fold that provoke the questions that Tevye cannot answer:

"You have a quotation for everything. Maybe you also have a quotation that explains why men have divided themselves up into Jews and gentiles, into lords and slaves, noblemen and beggars?"

"Now, now, my daughter, it seems to me you've strayed into the *'sixth millenium.'* " And I explained to her that this had been the way of the world since the first day of Creation.

"And why," she wanted to know, "should this be the way of the world?"

"Because that's the way God created the world."

"And why did God create the world in this way?"

"If we started to ask why this, and wherefore that, '*there would be no end to it*—a tale without end.' "

"But that is why God gave us intellects," she said, "that we should ask questions."

"We have an old custom," I told her, "that when a hen begins to crow like a rooster, we take her away to be slaughtered. As we say in the morning blessing, 'Who gave the rooster the ability to discern between day and night. . . .' "

Tevye is not equipped for this debate. His proverbial threat against the woman who begins to act like a man and the loosely associated quotation from the blessing are inadequate answers. The questions Chava asks stand outside the range of debate as Tevye knows it. Tevye's daughters are at once and for the same reasons the source of his pride and his anguish.

If the major burden attached to the blessing of seven daughters is the provision of seven dowries, there might be compensation in a few "good" marriages. This is Tevye's dream, a dream from which he is repeatedly retrieved by accident, poverty, and the independent will of his daughters. When it appears that Tsaytl is betrothed to the wealthy butcher Leyzer-Volf, Tevye stretches out in his wagon and lets his horse be his guide while he indulges in his own version of utopian fantasy:

I shall yet have joy—*nakhes fun meyn kind,* [a formula that refers to the honors that are to be derived from one's children] I shall know what it is to visit my child and find her a mistress of a well-stocked home, with chest full of linens, pantries full of chicken fat and preserves, coops full of chickens, geese and ducks. . . .

Suddenly my horse dashes off downhill, and before I can lift my head to look around I find myself on the ground with all my empty pots and crocks and my cart on top of me.

Tevye is by no means interchangeable with the luckless paupers whom we have met in other stories, but he shares with them the tendency to shuttle back and forth between an ideal dream world and disastrous reality represented here by the imagined ascent and real fall.

In the later Tevye stories, those written after the turmoil of 1905, broad, public disaster tends to take the place of familial difficulties. The rich young man who betrays Schprintze (1907) comes to Boyberik in order to escape pogroms elsewhere. Beilke marries when the world, as she thinks, is "back to where it was," but in the next and last story, "Get Thee Out" (1914), the world is again turned upside down. Tevye explains that he had set out for the Land of Israel at the behest of his son-in-law Padhatzur. Only the death of another son-in-law, Mottel Kamzoil, brought him back before he left Odessa to support the widow, Tsaytl, and her children. With one foot in the Land of Israel he is retrieved again. "The Holy Land is over there and I am still here—'outside the Promised Land.'. . . I have always been a shlimazl and a shlimazl I will die." His trip was premature. Tevye is called back to take his place in the diaspora along with other luckless Jews.

God, says Tevye, likes to play with us. Even Padhatzur, the rich son-in-law, has fallen. "Who raiseth up the poor out of the dust," says Tevye, recalling for us the headnote of the first story, also brings us down. Thus God plays. *Aroyf un arop,* up and down. The times are bad and no one is immune. Once again Jews are being driven from the villages, and now it is Tevye's turn. At another time, he recalls, his Russian neighbors came to him under obligation to do some damage to their Jew. What if an official were to come by and find that they had left a Jew unharmed? It is agreed that they need only break a few windows. "Is Tevye right when he says that we have a great and merciful God?. . .They came to curse and they remained to bless." Having been "blessed" with the lesser of two evils at that time, Tevye now finds himself in worse times from which there is no release. "It was in the days of Mendel Beilis. . . ." Hard times bring thoughts of the Messiah:

Lord, Lord, I thought, what times these are! What is the world coming to? And where is God, the ancient God of Israel. Why is He silent? Wherefore does He permit such things to happen. . . . What is this world? And the next world? And why doesn't the Messiah come? Wouldn't it be clever of him to appear at this very moment riding on his white horse. . . . It seems to me that he has never been so badly needed by our people as now. . . . Our eyes are strained from watching. He is our only hope. All we can do is hope and pray for this miracle—that the Messiah will come.

When Tevye looks up he sees a man approaching on a white horse but it is not the Messiah. It is the bearer of more bad news. "Haman approacheth.—When you're waiting for the Messiah, the village constable comes riding." The constable tells Tevye that he is to leave within three days. All of the villages in the area are being cleared of the Jews. Zolodievke, Rabilevke, Kostolomevke, even Anatevke which has always been a town has become a village for the purposes of eviction. "And you, Tevel, pack up your things and go, go to Berdichev."

The village constable replaces the herald of the Messianic age, and when he speaks to Tevye he speaks a version of the words of God to Abraham, *Lekh-lekho,* as the story is called, "Get thee out."

The Lord said to Abram, "Leave your own country, your kinsmen, and your father's house and go to a country that I will show you. I will make you into a great nation, I will bless you and make your name so great that it shall be used in blessings. (Gen. 12: 1-2)

Of course, when Abraham—or Abram as he was then called—received this message it came with the promise of the establishment and expansion of his people in the land of Canaan. The same injunction sends Tevye in the opposite direction, further into exile. But it is the peculiarity of Jewish history (which recreates itself in these stories) that the original covenant is a source of endless pride to the Jews. Every manifestation of the covenant, often a cause for wonder, is potentially a cause for laughter. The first of these is God's promise of a son to Abraham's aged wife:

Both Abraham and Sarah had grown very old, and Sarah was past the age of child-bearing. So Sarah laughed to herself. . . . The Lord said to Abraham, "Why did Sarah laugh and say, 'Shall I indeed have a child when I am old?' Is anything impossible for the Lord?" (Gen. 18:11-14)

By the covenant the Jews were chosen and no amount of suffering thereafter removes that special condition. Rather, suffering seems to confirm it. Tevye is proud to be among the chosen. A history of continual suffering confirms the choice. This central paradox accounts for the most profound and consistent strain of comedy in Sholom Aleichem.

As long as Tevye is able to see his tribulations as a result of the same divine whimsy that assured the birth of Isaac and continued to confirm the covenant to the Jews of the Bible, his own comedy continues. In Tevye's famous complaints, especially those addressed to God, we hear the essential elements of this comedy:

Azoi hot er zikh geshpielt mit Tevye: *oylim viyordim*—aroyf un arop!
   Thus has He played with Tevye: *up and down*, up and down!

Tevye is God's plaything, but the Hebrew words that he uses to describe his rise and fall—*oylim viyordim*—are the words used to describe the angels ascending and descending the ladder in Jacob's dream before the lord repeats the covenant (Gen. 28:12). And again in the last story:

"Ah, dear God, our Father," I thought, "Why do You always have to pick on Tevye to do Thy will? Why don't You make sport of someone else for a change? A Brodsky, for instance, or a Rothschild? Why don't You expound to them the lesson *Lekh-lekho*—Get thee out? It seems to me that it would do them more good than me. In the first place they would find out

what it means to be a Jew. In the second place, they would learn that we
have a great and mighty God.''

The fact that Tevye and not Brodsky is God's chosen plaything is a
source of pride for Tevye. It confirms his Jewishness. The rich do
not know ''what it means to be a Jew.'' Being forced to move from
the place where you have always lived is undeniably a cause for sorrow, and that sorrow is not hidden from the reader. But when
Tevye explains to his weeping daughter that they share their eviction with other Jews his speech falls under the auspices of the comic
paradox:

''What do you think I am—God's favorite son? Am I the only one chosen
for this honor? Aren't other Jews being driven out of the villages
too? . . . Even your Anatevke which has been a town since the world began has, with God's help, become a village too, all for the sake of the few
Jews who live there. Are we any worse off than all the others?''

Each of Tevye's locutions is controlled by his recognition of the
paradoxical place of suffering in Jewish history. Eviction becomes
an ''honor'' which is extended to Anatevke ''for the sake'' of the
Jews there. Tevye is convinced that it is a privilege to be a Jew even
when this privilege is proved through suffering. This conviction allows him to pretend that lamentation is a luxury. In ''Modern
Children'' he tells the same daughter not to weep over the proposed
marriage to Leyzer-Volf. ''Look, you've cried enough for one
day. . . . Even eating pastry becomes tiresome.'' Under the conditions that we would take to be normal—that is, nonparadox-
ical—we would not accept the comparison of tears with pastry any
more than we would accept the pride of the pauper cited above.
Judaism provides the conditions which allow the simultaneous,
paradoxical expression of the pathetic and the comic.

In ''Get Thee Out'' the pathetic appearance of the cat that they
must abandon in their travels prefigures the appearance of the repentant apostate, Chava. When all the packing is finished, the cat
sits ''looking as lonely and forsaken as an orphan.'' When Tevye
points to the cat—''she too is to be pitied''—Tsaytl raises the issue
of Chava who has returned and wishes to join the family.

''The moment she found out that we were being sent away she swore to
herself that if we were driven out, she would go too. That's what she told

me herself. Our fate is her fate, *unzer goles—dos iz ihr goles,* our exile is her exile.''

"Exile" in this case does not simply mean removal from a particular location. The Yiddish *goles*—or Hebrew *galut*—refers to the long separation of the Jews from the Land of Israel. It represents the geographic dislocation as well as a spiritual separation from God that will be concluded with the coming of the Messiah. *Goles* defines the time and the space and the spiritual condition in which the Jew wanders on this side of redemption. When Tevye receives Chava back into his family he also confers on her what he might call the privilege of joining them in further exile. Since the destruction of the Temple a large part of the Jewish identity has been formed in the *goles.* The Yiddish language is one example of that formation. At the same time life in the *goles* has meant a continual assault on Jewishness. Thus Tevye is able to see his further wandering under the heading of God's command to Abraham as a confirmation of his Jewishness, another in the long series of disasters which is to precede the arrival of the Messiah. In his final valediction Tevye tells Sholom Aleichem that he does not know where he is going, maybe Odessa, maybe Warsaw, maybe even America:

"Unless the Almighty, the Ancient God of Israel, should look about him suddenly and say to us, 'Do you know what, my children? I shall send the Messiah down to you.' . . . *Unzer alter Got lebt,* our ancient God still lives!''

Sholom Aleichem's comedy is like the Messianic promise. It converts all the evidence of *a paskudneh velt,* "a wretched world," into hopefulness and even levity. Against all proof Tevye finds reason to hope and in all manner of disaster he finds the occasion for a joke.

Of course Tevye is not Sholom Aleichem. In a headnote to the collected stories Sholom Aleichem tells us that his function is to record everything Tevye says "word for word." Thus he leaves the impression that he is the writer-as-scribe rather than the author of the stories. The folk writer listens to the popular voice and records what he hears. We receive these stories with the knowledge that Sholom Aleichem too is listening, and we record his unspoken judgment. When we consider Tevye's words from this additional distance, we find further cause to smile at—not so much with—his assumption of the Messianic idea. Gershom Sholem has said that "the magnitude of the Messianic idea corresponds to the endless powerlessness in Jewish history during all the centuries of exile." Power is replaced with hope. "There is something profoundly unreal about it."[25] Readers laugh at what is unreal in the lives of Sholom Aleichem's paupers. Laughter may bring with it an awareness of its cause, the lamentable gap between the real and the imagined life of the comic hero. After awareness comes action. Zionists and socialists would absorb the lore of Sholom Aleichem even as they set out to change the conditions that made his comedy possible.

CHAPTER 4

The Speaking Voice

I N his essay on Nikolai Leskov, Walter Benjamin describes the historical process that "has quite gradually removed narrative from the realm of living speech and at the same time is making it possible to see a new beauty in what is vanishing."[1] The printing press and the vast expansion of its use along with other advances of industrialism had already made storytelling obsolete along the Atlantic fringe of Europe and North America toward the end of the nineteenth century. On the fringes of this world, in Russia and in frontier America, several writers found ways of telling stories in print without losing the charm of "living speech." Benjamin discusses Leskov. Mark Twain is another and so is Sholom Aleichem.

Storytelling was still very much alive among Jews of the Russian Pale in Sholom Aleichem's time, and many of his own stories take the form of a spoken tale. In "On Account of a Hat" the writer, Sholom Aleichem, listens while another man, a Kasrilevkite, tells him the story of Sholom Shakhnah. Continual interjections—"do you hear me?"—remind us that the Kasrilevkite and not Sholom Aleichem is responsible for the story. At the end when the man asks his question—"You think it's so easy to put one over on Kasrilevke?"—we are left with the final reminder that what we have read is a spoken communication between two people and that one of them, the speaker, lives on the same plane with everyone else in Kasrilevke, including the subject of his story, Sholom Shakhnah. It is only the speaker's arrogance that separates him from the *shlimazl* in the story. Otherwise he is one of the people, speaking with the identifiable voice of the people. The identification of the speaker in the frame and the way he speaks when he takes over combine to place the story within the circle of folk culture. He tells Sholom Aleichem that he has "bushels and baskets of stories"

95

about Sholom Shakhnah. His story emerges from a folk anthology available to any citizen of Kasrilevke. The verbal tics of the speaker do not give the story a particular style or signature by which we generally identify writers. Rather these tics are the earmarks of a typical storyteller who relates his stories aloud without benefit of correction or "style." He is, as Sholom Aleichem assures us in the frame, "no *litterateur.*" A story belongs to literature when "an author puts down his completed piece of writing." It belongs to folklore "from the moment it is adopted by the community."[2] Even while Sholom Aleichem was in the act of making Yiddish into a vehicle for a written literature, he deliberately left the impression of the opposite process in his stories. The apparent dominance of the speaking voice constitutes an escape from literature into folkways through a mode of narration well known to Russian writers and best identified by Russian critics as *skaz*, a word meaning "to say, speak, relate."

As a form *skaz* creates the illusion of speech in stories where a large part of what we read is given over to what appears to be the transcription of one voice speaking. It is to be distinguished from literary I-narration by the presence of a listener within the frame of the story. When the second person is used it is this listener, not a vague reading public, that is intended. In what follows it will be convenient to refer to the literary, first-person narration as "narration" and to *skaz* as "speech." We are constantly made aware that what we read is intended to be speech by the way language is used, by the word order, the spelling, and the vocabulary. Often *skaz* is marked as speech and not narration by the use of dialect. Spelling can be made to indicate special pronunciation, though eccentric spelling is less frequent among the early Yiddish writers who were also charged with the standardization of the printed language. Word order and vocabulary are marked by their departure from standard usage. In what the speaker says the rigorous control of plot that we often associate with the short story gives way to the rambling and digressive patterns of natural speech, often in excess. The result is less a story than a characterization. The character of the speaker comes to us as it does in drama, through speech without benefit of authorial interpretation. If the author can be said to exist in the text of *skaz,* he resides in the second person, the listener, called by Mikhail Baxtine the "compositional equivalent" of the author, present perhaps in a frame story. Otherwise the author is effaced from the monologue, and yet we are aware of his shadowy presence as a listener and as an enlarged consciousness that allows us to judge the necessarily limited perspective of the speaker. This narrowness may simply be the limitation placed on a single point of view; it may also be a function of the geographical, social, and educational level implied by the use of dialect. Whatever the cause, the effect is ironic. Our bird's-eye view corrects what Victor Erlich calls the "worm's eye view" of the speaker. Erlich discusses *skaz* in a short article where he suggests that this notion could be fruitfully applied to the monologues of Sholom Aleichem. Earlier Russian critics studied Leskov and Gogol. American readers have met *skaz* in Mark Twain's "Celebrated Jumping Frog" and in Ring Lardner's "Haircut."[3]

Sholom Aleichem's sense of himself as an artist in a popular rather than strictly literary tradition helps to explain his affinity for this form of storytelling. The reason for this affinity is especially clear in the light of comments of Baxtine:

The element of *skaz* in the direct sense (an orientation toward oral speech) is a factor necessarily inherent in any storytelling. Even if the narrator is represented as writing his story and giving a certain literary polish to it, all the same he is not a literary professional; what he commands is not a specific style but only a socially or individually defined manner of storytelling, a manner that gravitates toward oral *skaz*. . . . We believe that in the majority of cases *skaz* is brought in precisely for the sake of a different voice, one which is socially distinct and carries with it a set of viewpoints and evaluations which are just what the author needs. In point of fact, it is a storyteller who is brought in, and a storyteller is not a literary man; he usually belongs to a lower social strata, to the common people (precisely the quality the author values in him), and he brings with him oral speech.[4]

The nonliterary orientation of *skaz* eases the transition from folkways into literary conventions for the Yiddish writer, and the oral presentation gives the Yiddish writer a vehicle that is especially appropriate to his language. Max Weinreich explains the use of Yiddish among Russian Jews in a way that shows how natural it is for this language to be assimilated into literature through the vehicle of *skaz*. He distinguishes the traditional literary language, Hebrew, from Yiddish:

Ashkenazic bilingualism, definitely, is not founded on the dichotomy of sacred versus profane. The difference it stresses is that between oral language and the language of recording. . . . Just as Hebrew was the language of recording, Yiddish was the language of speech. As soon as the businessmen, or the rabbis for that matter, met and went on discussing the issues raised in their [Hebrew] correspondence, the erstwhile Hebrew writers at once switched to Yiddish. Oral communication, except for passages from the sacred texts repeated verbatim, was firmly linked with the vernacular.[5]

Sholom Aleichem would exploit the illusion of oral speech to lay the base for the rise of a secular, vernacular literature among the Jews of eastern Europe.

I   *The American Example*

The characteristic features of *skaz* are dependent on features of language and style which are difficult to penetrate in a foreign language and even more difficult to translate. For this reason we will precede our study of Sholom Aleichem's use of this form with a look at two American examples. The style is most clearly identified and understood by the native speaker. It is our belief that a reader trained in native examples is then prepared to appreciate the foreign.

The American reader has been prepared for a reading of Sholom Aleichem's monologues by humorists whose work is allied to an oral, folk tradition. Mark Twain, the most notable American practitioner, was fully aware of the difficulties in translating the form that we are calling *skaz*. For the 1875 edition of "The Celebrated Jumping Frog" he affixed a French translation in order to prove this point. Translation into standard French flattens all that is distinct in Simon Wheeler's monologue. Mark Twain's deliberately maladroit retranslation of the French back into English is an amusing exercise, but it misrepresents the problems of translation. Wheeler's first words are:

"Rev. Leonidas W. H'm, Reverend Le—well, there was a feller once by the name of *Jim* Smiley, in the winter of '49—or maybe it was the spring of '50—I don't recollect exactly, somehow . . .

In the French:

"Il y avait une fois ici un individu connu sous le nom de Jim Smiley: c'était dans l'hiver de 49, peut-être bien au printemps de 50, je ne me rappelle pas exactement."

And back into English:

"It there was one time here an individual known under the name of Jim Smiley; it was in the winter of '49, possibly well at the spring of '50, I no me recollect not exactly.

What is to be done? A word for word translation of Simon Wheeler's speech is impossible; the rendition in standard French is dull, and a French equivalent may not exist.

The translator of Sholom Aleichem into English faces many of the problems of the foreign translator of Mark Twain, especially when he sets out to translate writing that purports to represent speech. The sense that the speaker is using Yiddish, often in an idiosyncratic way, must be retained without giving way to the parody suggested by the faithful recreation of Yiddish syntax in English. The reader of the Yiddish text will only find Yiddish syntax amusing in certain instances, and it is these instances that the translator must try to render. Similar problems accompany the other features of speech.

We can appreciate the problems faced by a foreign translator of "The Celebrated Jumping Frog." For Mark Twain the story came directly out of the oral, folk milieu. He first heard the story of the jumping frog as a tale told around a tavern stove in a mining camp. He told the story to a friend who recommended that he "write it down," as his biographer says.[6] A story that is "written down" instead of "written" suggests dictation, a transcription of a spoken tale in this case. "The Celebrated Jumping Frog" retains that quality in its final form. The narrator of the frame story acts as a listener and then as a recorder of Simon Wheeler's tale, which he hears without interruption and, we are to assume, records verbatim. The difference between a conventional first person or I-narration and *skaz* should be evident in a comparison of the first words of the narrator and the first words of the speaker: "In compliance with the request of a friend of mine, who wrote me from the East, I

called on good-natured, garrulous old Simon Wheeler, and in-
quired after my friend's friend, Leonidas W. Smiley, as requested
to do, and I hereunto append the results." After several paragraphs
of explanation, Simon Wheeler begins with the words already
quoted: "Rev. Leonidas W. H'm, Reverend Le—well . . ."
Wheeler is allowed to pause and reflect and correct himself. Unfinished words and sentences, indications of pronunciation and vocal
emphasis as well as the deictic "here" pointing to an immediate location of the speaker all depart from the standard first-person narration and contribute to the impression of speech.

Throughout his tale Simon Wheeler wanders through the same
maze indicated by his first sentence. A more direct response would
have been: "Leonidas W. Smiley. Never heard of him." Instead
Wheeler comes up with a *Jim* Smiley and sets out to prove that "he
was the curiousest man about always betting on anything." A number of examples of Smiley's obsessive gambling lead to the story of
the jumping frog. The proof is serial; that is, it takes the form of a
list with digressions. A list of this kind need never end. In this case
the monologue ends when Wheeler is called away and the listener
makes his getaway. Thus if we simplify Wheeler's digression we
have two stories represented by two distinct uses of language. The
story of the jumping frog exists within the frame of a story about a
man who is trapped by an incorrigible raconteur. The frame is a
first-person narration written in no particular place for no particular audience in a language reserved for written expression. Smiley
speaks to a particular listener within the boundaries of a particular
time and place. The fact that from what he says we could not then
say where or when he is speaking does not contradict our sense that
he is speaking at a definite location and at a certain time: "Just set
where you are, stranger, and rest easy—I ain't going to be gone a
second." We locate the scene from within. "Where you are"
becomes the place; "a second" is the time; "You . . . stranger" is
the listener. It is just these intimate indications of the immediate
scene that limit the perspective and make explicit indications of historical time and geographical place unlikely. The difference between a broad perspective and the narrow perspective of the
speaker within the scene makes room for the irony characteristic of
this form.

The double vision required by irony is first provided by the relation of frame and monologue. Even in the absence of an actual

frame story, as in Ring Lardner's "Haircut," the implied prescience of a listener adds another consciousness and with it the other mentality that stands between us and speaker and makes for irony. Frequently we are made to understand that this consciousness resides in the listener, the "compositional equivalent" of the author within the story.

The listener, though frequently silent, has an important role to play in the monologue. He is frequently a stranger. In Mark Twain's story he has connections in "the East," and in Lardner's story the listener is recognized as an outsider: "You're a newcomer, ain't you? I thought I hadn't seen you round before. I hope you like it good enough to stay. As I say, we ain't no New York City or Chicago, but we have pretty good times." He is a stranger, but he must in no way inhibit the loquaciousness of the speaker. He is enough of an insider to inspire confidence and enough of an outsider to require explanation. A complete insider would reduce the monologue to the inscrutable local code that passes for communication within a household or within the most intimate communities. The complete outsider would not understand the dialect or, in the case of Yiddish, the language. Our recognition of linguistic peculiarity creates boundaries between the speaker's world and our own. A person may be very much within the geographic and linguistic range of the speaker and still recognize peculiarities, which will create a sense of distance and, with it, a sense of irony. If we allow the idea of boundary to be represented by geography, the world that is familiar to the speaker in "Haircut" is limited to a few small towns in Michigan. Whitey refers to Detroit and "the Northern Penninsula" as the outer rim of his world. Beyond that rim are New York and Chicago, which are made to seem as familiar as the local towns mentioned in the monologue are unfamiliar. The microscopic geography that is known to the little people in the story is largely hidden to the outside world, and this difference is the difference in perspective that guides the irony of the story. From our vantage point we are allowed to be amused by the way local people talk, and we assume the enlarged moral stature that allows us to censure their moral pettiness.

Small-town Michigan was the place of Ring Lardner's youth. By the time he wrote "Haircut" he had moved away from Michigan, in fact, to Chicago and New York. It is not uncommon for the masters of this style to recreate the language and location known to

their youth from the vantage point of maturity. Sholom Aleichem
did the same in Odessa and Kiev and eventually in New York. In the
1920s American writers from the Middle West were still engaged in
the critical judgment of small-town life that began in Hannibal,
Missouri, and had been going on as long in the Russian Pale. At the
same time the American small towns were diminishing into railway
stops on the way to big cities, and local dialects were giving way to
the uniformity of mass communication. Ring Lardner would live to
be the satirist of the radio voice. With the diminution of regional
differences in America and the urbanization of the *shtetl* in Russia,
writers in both countries began "to see a new beauty in what [was]
vanishing" and to record it for the amusement as well as for the
budding nostalgia of their readers. This, to extend Benjamin's
point, is when "living speech" and storytelling work their way into
written literature.

The writing of *skaz* corresponds in some ways to the collecting of
folksongs and folktales insofar as collection generally begins when
the folk tradition is dying out. It is an attempt to salvage what is all
but lost to modernism. Some Yiddish writers—Peretz and An-
sky—engaged in the collection of folklore that definitely enters
their art. But can we say of Sholom Aleichem and Mark Twain that
they wrote folktales? Certainly characters like Tevye and Tom
Sawyer have entered folk tradition. If the stories themselves seem
to be folktales it is because they are framed and spoken in such a
way that they seem to emanate directly from the folk. Within explicit or implicit frames we meet nonliterary people who spin yarns
in a voice that we associate with speech and communication rather
than with literary narration. But the key to the folkloric quality of a
story is found in the form that it takes in repetition. A folktale is
retellable. Now when a story like "The Celebrated Jumping Frog"
is retold the qualities that are most likely to be lost are precisely
those that give us the impression that it comes to us directly from
the folk. The frame will be forgotten, and it is unlikely that the
dialect will be reproduced. For one thing dialect does not survive
indirect quotation. We may say:

"Wheeler says, 'He ketched a frog one day.' "

But we cannot say:

"Wheeler said that he ketched a frog one day."

Only a person who actually speaks Wheeler's dialect would report his speech in the second way. Otherwise the folk dialect only survives direct quotation, which is the way that oral *skaz* can survive intact. Thus its survival has more in common with the survival of a literary work than with the continuity of folklore:

A literary work is objectivized, it exists concretely apart from the reciter. Each subsequent reader or reciter returns directly to the work. Although the interpretation of previous reciters can be taken into account, this is only one of the components in the reception of the work; whereas for a folklore work the only path leads from implementer to implementer.[7]

So say Roman Jakobson and Petr Bogatyrev, writing in the wake of the formalist interest in a Russian literature that draws heavily on folklore. Sholom Aleichem and Mark Twain are not to be considered collectors of folklore nor are they what Jakobson and Bogatyrev call "implementers." Their stories often include folktales and they preserve the folk voice. For both the imitation of folklore is the triumph of art.

II   *The Yiddish Example*

Sholom Aleichem, like Mark Twain, was fond of reading his stories aloud. Both writers understood that the special quality of what they had written could best be conveyed with the speaking voice. Early in his career Mark Twain wrote to his wife that the "Jumping Frog" was "the best humorous sketch America has produced yet, and I must read it in public some day, in order that people may know what there is in it." For both writers the power of a story is in the presence of a speaking voice and much of what they write is geared to promote the conviction in the reader that he is not reading but listening.

Sholom Aleichem often seems to be telling rather than writing a story: "Listen, Jewish children, I will tell you a story about a little knife. . . ." Not only among children but among adults he repeatedly demonstrates the function of the storyteller. Storytelling is not reserved for specialists. We are reminded many times that anyone Sholom Aleichem meets is a possible raconteur, and in a number of stories he includes the telling of a tale in a way that shows the importance of storytelling among Jews of the Pale. For this he frequently adopts the format of the spoken tale implanted within a narrative. In addition to providing the occasion for the interior tale, the narrative frame is itself a story about what happens when a story is told. The teller of tales exercises definite powers over people, powers that may or may not be benign. As readers we are obliged to look closely at the act of storytelling within the stories of Sholom Aleichem.

In "The Tenth Man" a group of nine Jews in a railway car seeks the participation of a tenth to complete the *minyan* required for one of their number to say a mourner's prayer for his dead son.[8] The tenth man is an assimilated Jew, reluctant to join, but convinced to do so by another who says he will reward him with a good story. When the prayer is completed the storyteller tells three brief anecdotes that shame the tenth man and drive him out of the car at the next stop. The storyteller is especially important in the railway car, the forum *par excellence* in Sholom Aleichem. The railway brings a mixing of strangers, enforced idleness, a necessary suspension of business, and the convenient punctuation of stops. As we have seen, travel away from home is the frequent occasion of adventure. At the very least people meet, speak, and respond to each other in a way that is itself the action of a story.

In the *Railway Stories* the train brings the familiar author-listener together with the speakers whose stories he records. In "The Station at Baranovitch" the general chatter of disasters cited at the beginning of chapter 3 resolves itself into the telling of a single tale. The voice of a speaker interrupts the summary of the narrator. The long list of problems ends with the infamous name of Azev, the revolutionary terrorist and police agent known to English readers as Razumov in Conrad's *Under Western Eyes*. The interrupting voice picks this name out of the air and repeats it with his own eccentric pronunciation, "Aszhev." He has a tale of treachery that puts Azev in the shade. His pronunciation and his pauses remind us that we are reading the story of a man speaking to a crowd of Jews on a train as well as listening to a story about an innkeeper who is helped to escape from prison and punishment by his generous townsmen. From abroad the innkeeper sends more and more outrageous requests for help, finally blaming his benefactors for his exile. Chief among these benefactors is the speaker's grandfather whose plight is the subject of the story. Eventually the ingrate, having received money at every request, tries outright blackmail. He will tell the officials how he escaped if the grandfather does not send more money. At each stage of the storytelling, as the tension mounts with every request, the speaker tantalizes his listeners by pausing for a cigarette or leaving the car for something to eat at a station buffet. During these pauses we return to the narrator who describes the tension among the anxious audience. As readers we respond both to the speech act that takes place on the train as an event in itself and to the series of events that the speaker describes. Both are exasperating. When and how will it end? Finally in the station at Baranovitch, when the story seems to have reached its crisis, the speaker jumps up, announces that he has reached his destination, and leaves the train with his story unfinished and his audience unsatisfied. We have come to regard storytelling in two ways, but on reflection we see that both stories are essentially the same. It is as if a con man for reasons of his own were to tell a story about a con man.

In "The Station at Baranovitsh" part of the confidence trick lies in the speaker's ability to convince his audience that only he could finish the story. When he begins to speak everyone in the car is sure he has heard the story before, that it had happened in his town, but the speaker assures them that it is all historical fact, once recorded in his town hall which, unfortunately, burned down with all of its records. The kind of story told by the traveler is a familiar folktale which really belongs to the community of listeners. What the listeners do not know is how it will be concluded in this case, and before they can find out, this story gives way to another story, the story of how a trainload of Jews was cheated of a conclusion. The story reminds its readers of the place the storyteller takes in the community of Jews. It was certainly part of Sholom Aleichem's sense of his own place among his listeners that Baranovitsh is the town where his own reading tour was cut short by his illness in 1908 shortly before the story was written.

"Sixty-six," written a year later, is a story told in the same form. The title refers to a card game favored by a stranger, described by the narrator as "a respectable man, a traveling salesman like me."[9] In the course of describing his own addiction to cards the stranger tells a number of anecdotes about other addicts who have been fleeced by strangers on trains. Finally, he describes the time that he himself was the victim of a team that pretended to be a father and a son. In the story the son plays foolishly at first, draws the speaker in, and then takes him for all he has. When they arrive in Odessa and the speaker realizes that he has been duped, the young man disappears and the old man remains to deny every claim of the victim who is made to seem mad. The story has by this time taken so many turns that we may have forgotten the brief frame in which it is lodged. We may be reading the story on only one level, attending only to the frustration and loss of the speaker, until we return to the frame narration at the very end. Having finished his series of stories, the speaker pulls out a deck of cards and suggests a game. The narrator, noting the ease with which his companion handles cards, brushes him off. The storytelling was the ploy of a con man softening up a victim. The reader is consciously or unconsiously obliged to anatomize the act of storytelling, to disengage the constituent parts of the story. The fact that both ''Sixty-six'' and ''The Station at Baranovitch'' point to a confidence game serves to emphasize both the doubleness and the possible duplicity of stories that divide themselves into two verbal acts, one that we are calling speech, the other narration.

The doubleness of these two stories can be seen simply as a division of intention. The speaker within the story has one intention or outright design on his listeners. He is prepared to trick them in one way or another with his storytelling. *Skaz* becomes performance. However repetitious and wayward the telling, we come to recognize the design of the speaker. This recognition becomes part of a second intention, that of the author speaking through his ''compositional equivalent,'' the listener and recorder. The author's intention is to tell a story about a certain act of storytelling. In the stories collected under the heading *Monologn (Monologues)* this doubleness is less obviously a question of the speaker's malign intention. The speakers in the monologues have no conscious design on their listeners. They are not tricksters. To start with they may be seeking advice, as in ''The Little Pot'' and ''A Bit of Advice,'' though it becomes clear that they do not mean to take it. Mostly they speak from a compulsion to speak. Speech takes the form of complaint. The obvious self-interest of the speaker in ''Sixty-six'' becomes a less conscious urge toward self-esteem. The speakers grope through indirection and repetition toward a recuperation of losses. They aim vaguely at self-aggrandizement, and they never succeed. ''Gitl Purishkevitch'' is trapped in the endless maze of czarist bureaucracy in an attempt to free her only son from the draft; the man in

"A Predestined Disaster" is the victim of what appears to be appalling ingratitude from a family whose troubles he has inherited. Both defend themselves to the point where we as readers lose patience and turn our criticism away from the inequity that is being described to the process by which it is being described. In the end the speaker may force us to adopt the position of an absent antagonist, the bureaucrat, the neighbor, the child who is the apparent occasion of the complaint. From the point of view of original intention, the speech backfires; it has no other effect than to confirm and compound the predicament of the speaker. In two stories where advice is sought the supplicants succeed only in antagonizing their potential benefactors, a rabbi in "The Little Pot" and Sholom Aleichem, the author, in "A Bit of Advice."[10]

In "The Little Pot" Yente goes to the rabbi to ask if the pot that she has reserved for the cooking of meat has been made nonkosher by the spilling of a pot of milk in the same oven. She arrives at her question only after a long series of seemingly unrelated complaints and observations, bits of gossip and recrimination and, for her son, undiluted praise—all that has made the name Yente synonymous with talk. The rabbi is overwhelmed. Although we do not hear a word from him, he finally faints and the monologue ends with Yente's cry for the *rebbetzin* and water. We have here the characteristic double-story line, but the emphasis in "The Little Pot" falls squarely on the speech act itself. Neither the frame story of a rabbi who is talked to distraction nor the speaker's story of a contaminated pot is particularly important to the reader's response to the monologue. The pot is barely mentioned, and the fainting fit is just a convenient way to turn off what could be an endless flow of speech. The speech is everything, and it is the peculiar progress within Yente's sentences and then from subject to subject that draws and keeps the reader's attention.

The speech that overwhelms the rabbi is a rapid patter of language back and forth through repetitions and inversions that turn nearly every sentence into a pattern of balanced phrases that mount and progress through the addition of more words. She begins by introducing her problem in a forthright way: "Rabbi! Ikh vill aykh fregen a shalleh vill ikh aykh" (Rabbi! I want to ask you a question want I to [ask] you). Already we note a dangerous tendency to prolixity. The balanced parentheses of pronoun-verb-verb-pronoun betray her natural tendency toward a rhythm of speech that approaches song and demands return and repetition. She continues:

> Ikh bin Yente bin ikh, Yente di Kurelapnitshke.
> Ikh handel mit eyer handel ikh,
> mit eyfes, mit genz, un mit katshkes.
> Ikh hob mir mayne shtendige kaynetes, hob ikh mir.

> I am Yente am I, Yente the Poultrywoman.
> I deal in eggs deal I,
> in chickens, in geese, in ducks.
> I have my regular customers have I.

Each additional line continues the pattern of redundancy. Yente is Yente the Poultrywoman; by definition pountrywomen deal in eggs, chickens, geese, and ducks. Yente's life is like her speech in that a great deal of energy is expended with little to show for it. Her speech is a treadmill made to work double time:

> Khap ikh a dreyerel, khap ikh,
> a mol do a mol dorten
> do genumen, dort gegeben, dort gegeben, do genumen—
> me' drayt zikh . . .

> Grab I three kopeks grab I,
> sometimes here sometime there,
> here take, there give, there give, here take—
> one turns about . . .

Repetitive phrases grow by the accretion of new words that stimulate new associations. Having introduced herself and described the way she makes a living and what kind of a living she makes she explains that she must work double time because she is a widow, but she knows what work is because when she was young she worked with her mother who was called Basheh, Basheh the Candlemaker, she was a candlemaker: "Meyn mama . . . Basheh hot zi gehaysen, Basheh di Lekhtsiherin, zi iz geven a lekhtsiherin. . . ." In those days candles were used and not these new lamps with the faulty chimneys which reminds her of the chimney she cracked last week. So it goes. She catches herself: "Yo, akegen vos iz dos gekumen tsu der?" (O, how did we get around to that?). This is the habitual phrase by which she recalls herself to what she believes to be her subject. Speakers in *skaz* are incorrigible wanderers whose most familiar verbal tics are the phrases by which they get back on the track.

Once back on the track Yente returns to the early death of her husband, which followed a cough that was very poorly diagnosed by the doctors who were also mistaken in the case of Yokel, son of Aaron the *Shokhet*. She, to return to the subject, is a widow left with a house to share with tenants, one a deaf old man and the other a flour dealer named Gnessi and her husband and children. Gnessi is a shrew who nags her husband and keeps a sloppy house, *fartiopet un farshliopet,* a real mess. Proverbial and homely speech makes this frequent appeal to rhyme. Her own cleanliness merits more emphatic rhyme:

> bay mir iz reyn, bay mir is sheyn,
> bay mir iz tsikhtig, bay mir iz likhtig

which shorn of rhyme means clean, lovely, immaculate, bright.

Gnessi's children are uncontrollable rascals, always clambering about the oven, just the opposite of her own Dovidl, the orphan, a scholar and sickly. The boy is the image of his father. He studies and coughs. She lists all of his accomplishments and all of his ailments. Once he was sick for six weeks when he was frightened by what he took to be a ghost but what turned out to have been Lippa the Water Carrier coming home at dusk in a white fur coat. Yente exercised all the folk customs that are known to prevent death—she spoke magic words over him, sold him and bought him back again, changed his name with the addition of Chaim, meaning life. Her account is passionate and pathetic. Here her propensity for crude rhythm and rhyme takes a sad, lyric turn: "un treren—treren, ver redt fun treren?" (and tears—tears, who speaks of tears?) After his sickness Yente is required by the doctor to give Dovidl hot chicken soup made from at least a quarter of a chicken every day. The heroic acquisition of this quarter chicken brings to mind the books that she also gets for him in spite of the doctor's recommendation that he read less. Clearly something is happening that Yente does not understand. David goes to *kheder* all day and reads all night. But what does he read? She does not know. She cannot read. He gives her lists of books to borrow from her rich customers. The doctor tells her that the boy must not stay up all night with these books.

"If he is fated to be a doctor, tell him he'll become a doctor a few years later." "What kind of a nightmare is that?" Yente asks herself. "Why not a governor?" When she tells her son what the doctor has said, he blushes fiercely and asks that they change doctors. "Don't even talk to him anymore." As far as Yente knows, her boy is bound for the yeshiva and religious study. But the doctor has seen David's books and knows otherwise. Again a new world creeps in, children change, and parents are left in the dark. The basic irony that surrounds *skaz* resides in the limited information of the speaker and the absence of any other point of view but for what enters through oblique allusion.

In spite of the apparent digression and repetition Yente is beginning to advance on her subject. It is the making of David's soup that is the occasion for the visit to the rabbi. One day Gnessi chooses to make dumplings—*balabekhkes*—with milk on the shared stove. Yente pauses for a little disquisition on Gnessi's cooking before she returns to the fatal hour. Gnessi's husband returns home early, they quarrel, and in the middle of things, the milk is spilt. A flurry of curses follows. David's soup is ruined. No great loss. Yente has a few other things around the house. But what of the pot? She has only one. Once she had three. She is in the act of describing the demise of the other two when the rabbi faints.

It is clear that Yente's case could be stated more simply. She emits a full-scale *apologia pro sua vita* where a brief statement would have been sufficient. It is characteristic of Sholom Aleichem's monologists that they reach toward broad confession or complaint no matter what the occasion. And yet the selection is not entirely random. Yente's speech is a thesis without a thesis sentence; it is an argument that hinges on hidden principles. In "Haircut" every detail contributes to an explanation of Jim Kendall's death, and yet it is not clear that the speaker fully understands what he has said. He gives us all the information that we need to know that Paul Dickson killed Kendall as punishment for shaming Julie Gregg and that Doc Stair uses his job as coroner to cover up the murder. Similarly all of Yente's digressions contribute to an explanation of the domestic chaos in which the crisis occurs. Extenuating circumstances may influence the rabbi's decision. She certainly wants to hear that her pot can be used again. Even if the pot has been contaminated, the process by which it can be made kosher again is not difficult.[11] But, as Zborowski and Herzog add, "running to the rabbi is time consuming and difficult." Surely Yente is seeking a favorable judgment, and yet we cannot be sure that she has exercised any conscious control over what she has said. As to her son, she says more than she fully understands. Ultimately a sense of order may be shared by the author and the reader but it is not known to the speaker and may be lost on the listener. The listener may know better, but the speaker is lost in a maze, and we are above it. The difference between the speaker's knowledge and ours is a condition of the irony that controls Sholom Aleichem's monologues.

When we speak of an author and a reader of *skaz* we refer to creatures whose existence cannot be inferred from the text. What the text gives us instead is a dialogue where one person assumes the role of speaker and the other of listener. We have said that in this process the effaced author becomes something more akin to the listener than the speaker. Sholom Aleichem assumes that role in one of the monologues and in the Tevye stories.

In "A Bit of Advice" a young man comes to Sholom Aleichem precisely because he is "such a prolific writer." As it happens, the advice that he seeks is not literary. He assumes rather naively that a prolific writer will know everything there is to know about life, and it is about his life that he wishes to be advised. But before Sholom Aleichem comes to understand the nature of the visit, he assumes that the young man is a writer with a manuscript in hand. The frame of a *skaz* narrative becomes a vehicle for explicit literary criticism. The beleaguered writer guesses that he will be subjected to a novel in three parts, "as long as the Jewish Exile," or a drama in four acts with characters who bear conveniently allegorical names, or an elevated ode to Zion with a quatrain that he offers up as parody. In other words, he names everything but the short story that adheres to everyday experience written in everyday Yiddish. This event, Sholom Aleichem seems to say, is the source of his own stories. Storytellers come to him like uninvited guests; they hail him on the road; they sit down next to him on railway trains. They speak to him, and he writes down what he hears.

In the course of asking whether or not he should divorce his wife, the young man in "A Bit of Advice" reveals all of his own snobbery, jealousy, and avarice and most of all his inability to accept advice or make a decision. The young man's chronic indecision is reflected by his inability as a speaker to say what he means: "I happen to be a young man from a little village. I mean, the village isn't such a little village, it's a rather good-sized village, one could very well say a town—but on the other hand, compared to your town, it is still a village." All this goes into the choice of *shtetl* or *shtodt,* a distinction that might be important if he were discussing rights of residence with a Russian official but which means nothing here. This indecision follows him through the story. When Sholom Aleichem gives him the advice that he has sought, the young man cannot follow it and reverses his position. Sholom Aleichem tries to accommodate him and is met with another reversal and then another and another until the writer rises in a fury and tries to throw his visitor out.

The narrator of this story is the listener but he is not simply the "compositional equivalent" of the author. Insofar as the story is by Sholom Aleichem we are to think of the narrator as the author or at least as a writer. In that case what the persistent speaker interrupts is the proper work of the writer which is not the giving of marital advice but the writing of stories. The young man's misconception of that task constitutes an impertinent imposition which he prolongs with his exasperating tendency to digress and his inability to make a decision. Several times Sholom Aleichem tries to force the young man to come to the point: "'If you don't mind, young man,' I interrupted him in midsentence." This variation of the uninterrupted speech is the author's joke at the expense of his own favored medium. His art is no contrivance; it is the irrepressible popular voice that accosts him and imposes itself upon him through no fault of his own.

In his best known sequence of stories Sholom Aleichem describes a far more congenial relation with his equally irrepressible friend Tevye. Little need be said about the relationship of Tevye and Sholom Aleichem in these stories. The frames are of very little importance as stories; the authorial figure, Sholom Aleichem, is almost totally effaced. His shadowy, silent presence and his identification as a writer of books account for the form of the stories. In the early stories the two men meet in vaguely specified or unspecified places and Tevye begins to speak. Tevye uses their infrequent and accidental meetings as the occasion for an explanation of what has happened in the interval. As the stories become more gloomy Tevye's premature aging is what requires explanation. When he comes to the story of Chava, the apostate, Tevye enjoins his friend not to repeat what he is about to tell him:

I would not repeat it to anyone else, for while the pain is great, the disgrace is even greater. But how is it written? *"Shall I conceal it from Abraham —Can I keep any secrets from you?"* Whatever is on my mind I shall tell you. But one thing I want to ask you. Let it remain between you and me. For I repeat: the pain is great, but the disgrace—the disgrace is even greater.

When he has concluded his story he repeats his request: "Be as silent as the grave concerning this. Don't put what I told you into a book." It may be a sign of Tevye's utter desolation at this point that even his confidential friend betrays him by recording his shame, but we would not say that "Chava" is the story of that betrayal. Sholom Aleichem's candor is at best a minor confirmation of the impression that the story derives from an extraliterary source. The last two stories are in part travel stories. Sholom Aleichem and Tevye meet while traveling, and Tevye must describe the events that uprooted him. "Tevye Goes to Palestine," written in the period of the *Railway Stories,* brings them together in a train compartment, but unlike "The Station at Baranovitch" and "Sixty-six" the encounter contributes very little to the total effect of the story. If the frames are unimportant in the Tevye stories, the fact that there is a listener is very important. The Tevye stories are to be regarded as speech; speech requires a listener. In order to give the impression of locution one must preserve the idea of an interlocutor, however silent. The presence of the listener is the occasion for the speaking voice, and it is through the preservation of the speaking voice that Sholom Aleichem was able to make a living literature out of the "jargon."

Nearly every sentence in the Tevye stories is impressed with the rhythm of spoken Yiddish and the peculiar wealth of allusion that characterizes the speaker. Tevye is fond of quotation, and his speech is most lively when he is quoting himself. Throughout the stories Tevye speaks to Sholom Aleichem, and much of what he says is quotation of what he has said at other times. When he tells Sholom Aleichem how he first gained the thirty-seven rubles from the grateful family in Boyberik, he recreates the scene outside the *datcha* where they live. The rich man turns to Tevye and asks who he is. "Where do you live. What do you do for a living? Do you

have any children? How many?'' Naturally Tevye lights on the last
question. His reply is filled with proverbs, unfinished Hebrew
phrases, quotations from prayer and from his wife put side by side,
all punctuated by the habitual "ikh zog . . . zog ikh" (I say).

Kinder? zog ikh. Nit tsu farzindiken. Oyb itlikher kind, zog ikh, iz verteh,
vi meyn Golde vill mir eynreden, a milyon, bin ikh reykher fun'm gresten
g'vir in Yehupetz. Der khesoren, zog ikh, vos orem iz nit reykh, krum iz
nit gleykh, azoi vi in posak shteyt: ha-mavdil bein koydish la-khoyl. Ver
es hot di klinger dem iz voyl.

Children? I say. Not to commit a sin [but] if each child, I say, is worth, as
my Golde wants to convince me, a million, I am richer than the richest
man in Yehupetz. The fault, I say, is that poor is not rich, crooked is not
straight, as it is written, "He who separates the sacred from the profane . . ." for the one with the coins things go well.

Tevye's response is never direct. In this case the abundance of
children is immediately associated with his poverty, the degree of
which is supported by a typically rhymed Yiddish proverb, the
truth of which is confirmed by the greater authority of a phrase
from Hebrew prayer. *Ha-mavdil bein koydish la-khoyl* comes from
the final prayer of the Sabbath, the *Havdalah,* marking the division
between the holy Sabbath and the profane week. This division is
now compared to the division of rich and poor, crooked and
straight, but the Hebrew phrase also reaches forward by rhyme into
the next phrase for *la-khoyl* in the Ashkenazic pronunciation
rhymes with the Yiddish *voyl.* In Tevye's speech sacred and profane are rarely divided. One flows into the other in fragments often
drawn together, as they are here, by rhythm and rhyme and free
association. Further along in the same speech he talks himself into
resignation: "God is a father. He has his way, that is, he sits above
and we suffer below. We labor, we drag logs; do we have any
choice?'' ''Vi di gemorah zogt: ba-makom she-ein ish—iz a hering
fish.'' (As the gemorah says: in a place where no man is—herring is
a fish.) It is true that gemorah refers to the place where no man is as
a place where whoever is there will have to serve, that is, have to become a man. Similarly wherever no other fish is available—that is,
among poor people—''herring is a fish,'' herring will do. Elliptical
phrases and eccentric connections draw the sacred and the profane
'ogether continually in Tevye's speech.

Tevye's insistent "zog ikh" calls repeated attention to the fact that this is speech, that this gymnastic verbosity is the result of a man speaking. We are reminded with every attribution of himself and every *b'kitzur* ("in short") that we are overhearing actual, extemporized speech. It is the total impression left by this style that makes it "hard to think of [Sholom Aleichem] as a 'writer'."

III *Written* Skaz

Skaz is, by definition, speech, and when we read it we read a text that pretends to be a transcription of speech and thus creates what Boris Eixenbaum called "the illusion of *skaz*." An earlier approach to an authentic use of language unmediated by the presence of an author created the epistolary novel, a form that has been given special favor by writers of *skaz*. Epistolary *skaz* differs very little from the speech act that it generally echoes. Much of the humor of the letter lies in the writer's inability to distinguish between written and spoken language. Words are spelled the way they sound. No concessions are made to prose style. Epistles in this style generally flow between two of a kind. Thus the characteristic silent listener in oral *skaz* is eliminated. The form continues to recreate an act of communication between a first and a second person, but the second person is allowed to respond in kind and is also subject to our sense of ironic distance.

Ring Lardner's "Some Like Them Cold" is a correspondence between a Mr. Lewis and a Miss Gillespie following a brief meeting at the train station in Chicago.[12] The letters pass between Chicago where she stays and New York where he has gone. We infer from the letters the story of their relationship which rises through a series of lures and flirtations and then vanishes when Mr. Lewis, who has become "Dear Mr. Man," finds another woman in New York and becomes "Dear Mr. Lewis" again. In the last letter she rebuffs him in a way that clearly terminates the series. It is amusing to see the way the relationship develops without narrative interpretation. Soon we project upon the letters our own sense of their direction and wait for the correspondents to catch on and adjust. What we see is two people pluming themselves with words, often falling flat in ways that neither recognizes. The writers characterize themselves through a series of written tics comparable to the repeated earmarks of oral *skaz*. Miss Gillespie uses quotation marks when she wishes to call attention to words that are not quite in her vocabulary: "Don't you love Service or don't you care for 'highbrow' writings?" The marks seem to mean that the word is on loan from somebody else; she is not entirely responsible for what she says within those marks. They never mean that she is quoting her correspondent. When she does cite something that he has said she expurgates it in a way that recommends her gentility. His comment on the heat of New York: "The reason why New Yorkers is so bad is because they think they are all ready in H——" meets her qualified approval: "I laughed when I read what you said about New York being so hot that people thought it was the 'other place.' " In his letters "girlies" or "pips" try to "make me" but he resists. She is "glad you have not 'fallen' for the 'ladies' who have tried to make your acquaintance in New York." When Mr. Lewis describes the woman that he is about to marry it is clear that he was not looking for the kind of refinement advertised by Miss Gillespie. In this case, "distants," as Mr. Lewis would write it, does not make the heart grow fonder, and letters are not enough.

The fragility of the epistolary relationship in Lardner's story is a function of the characteristic deviations from the standards of written prose. That is, both writers show that they would be more at home talking than writing. Mr. Lewis spells as he speaks, and Miss Gillespie requires quotation marks to render the tone of what she wants to say. The letters will not last. They should be talking to each other, not writing. Miss Gillespie is, by her own admission, "a great talker." Her sister "would be perfectly satisfied to just sit in the apartment and listen to me 'rattle on.' " Here the quotation marks seem to represent her sister's part in the dialogue. Written *skaz* records a yearning for speech.

Sholom Aleichem's Menakhem-Mendl stories take the form of several series of letters that pass between the husband who has taken temporary residence first in Odessa and then in Kiev and his wife Sheyne-Sheyndl in Kasrilevke.[13] We are not surprised to find that Mendl is first of all a talker. He describes his qualifications as an insurance salesman: "The most important thing is—language, the gift of speech. An agent has to know the language. That is to say, he has to know how to talk. Talk against time; talk at random; talk glibly, talk himself out of breath; talk you into things; talk in circles." For both husband and wife the will to speak overflows the boundaries of the letter into inevitable postscripts, and what they say poses obvious contradictions to the conventions of letter-writing. Both observe conventional salutations and valedictions of the kind that we also find in the correspondence between Sholom Aleichem and his father. Menakhem-Mendl begins:

To my dear, wise, and modest helpmeet, Sheyne-Sheyndl, long may she live!
Firstly, I am come to inform you that I am, by the grace of God, well and in good cheer. May the Lord, blessed be His name, grant that we always hear from one another none but the best, the most comforting, and the happiest of tidings—amen.

Often as not what follows is the report of an utter disaster, the happy tidings of another failure. Similarly Sheyne-Sheyndl begins: "To my dear, esteemed, renowned, and honored husband, the wise and learned Menakhem-Mendl, may his light shine forever." And she proceeds to decry him as an idiot. Her salutation continues: "In the first place, I want to let you know that we are all, praise the Lord, perfectly well, and may we hear the same from you, please God, and never anything worse." What she then says seems to exist in spite of what she has just said as a formal letter writer: "In the second place, I am writing to say that the children are down with the measles, all three of them, and I don't sleep nights, while he is sitting there drinking vinegar with licorice." Sometimes her habitual valediction is appropriate; sometimes it is not.

So please dash a telegram off to me, come home as soon as possible, and put an end to all this, which is the heartfelt wish of your really devoted wife, Sheyne-Sheyndl.

Rest assured that before you have time to look around, your partners will swindle you from head to foot, because you've always been a *shlimazl* and will remain a *shlimazl,* which is the heartfelt wish of your really devoted wife. . . .

What she really wants to say remains peculiarly detached from what she is obliged to write.
Sandwiched between the formal pieties of the introductions and conclusions are all of the peculiar tics and locutions that characterize the correspondents. Sheyne-Sheyndl calls attention to her husband's willful separation from his family by speaking to him as if she were speaking about him. "He is living happily ever after in

Odessa; he is riding around on springs, bathing in big and little fountains. . . . What else does he want!'' Her use of the third person recreates her own greatest fear, that other people are talking about them. It is also a way of recreating the conversations that go on between her and her mother whose responses to Mendl are constantly quoted by her daughter. ''Vi zogt di Mama'' (as mother says), is the phrase that repeatedly opens the maternal store of proverbs.

Phrases that recur in Menakhem-Mendl's letters all serve to reflect the conditions of his life. He is what is called a *luftmensh,* he lives on air, especially in Yehupetz where his aerial existance is enforced by police restrictions which do not allow him as a Jew to reside within the city. Every night he disappears to Boyberik or, later, to a rooming house where frequent raids send him into hiding. During the day he lives on the streets, harassed by the police when he cannot afford to sit in a cafe and be harassed by impatient waiters. He chases after a living on the fringe of the bourse, does his business on the streets and at cafe tables; he is constantly on the move. He lives among a whole population of Jews whose basic instability draws them to fly-by-night schemes. One must get rich quick or not at all. The speed and mobility of the life accounts for the haste in which the letters are written. ''And since I am pressed for time, I must cut this short,'' he writes toward the conclusion of each, before the valediction and the inevitable postscript.

All of Mendl's schemes begin with high hopes and end in disaster. We are given a foretaste of the fall with the phrases that accompany every dream vision: ''eyn khesoren iz nokh; iz ober di tsoreh . . .'' (There's only one problem, one drawback . . .). In one letter both phrases appear and thus impose two conditions that would make a deal impossible if it were not already a swindle. He has a chance to sell some valuable land. The first problem is that it is somewhere in Siberia—''Simber'' to Mendl—beyond the reach of railroads; the second problem is the want of a customer. Only Brodsky could afford it, and Brodsky is unapproachable. The role that Mendl is to take in these recurrent pipedreams is that of the middleman, and it is in the middle that he is always caught, ''un ikh oykh b'sukhm'' (and I among them): ''Manufacturers are pining away for a penny, capitalists are holding back, and brokers are out of a job, *un ikh oykh b'sukhm.*''

Menakhem-Mendl and Sheyne-Sheyndl are bound to repeat the

pattern of their letters through each cycle of adventures. Mendl's
hopes are high; his wife is skeptical; Mendl's hopes are crashed to
bits; his wife's fears are confirmed and she admonishes him to give
up and come home. Sometimes he heads for Kasrilevke, but generally even before that he has landed on another opportunity. He
speculates in the fluctuation of currency; he is a broker in houses
and forests and oil fields; he tries to be a writer, a marriage broker
and an insurance agent. Mendl's Messiah is money, and his
Messianic vision is definitely apocalyptic. Therefore nothing can
destroy his hopes. His great expectations seem to thrive on destruction, and in his letters the exaggeration of one spawns the other.
The letters are an exercise in superlative despair and its twin, hope:

I want you to know, my dearest wife, that the end of the world has come!
The rates of exchange which arrived from Petersburg are so terrible that
everything went dark before our eyes. It hit us like a bolt of lightning, like
a bomb. . . . The speculators have fled, disappeared into thin air, *un ikh
oykh b'sukhm*. The stock market is finished! . . . It's like the destruction
of the Temple!

By the postscript of the same letter despair is turned about: "After
your house burns down, you're bound to get rich. I believe that's
true, and after the kind of catastrophe we've had, one could do
wonderful business." As readers we tend to correct Mendl's turbu-
lent flights. The letters are written with an imperfect knowledge of
the world. When he writes he does not know the sequel of the events
that he describes. He is in the middle of them. Only the amusing
story of his career as a matchmaker is told as one long narrative
where he, as both the teller of the tale and its protagonist, must
withold the surprise ending. Otherwise the stories are split into letters written during the course of the events they describe. The
timing of events within this format limits his knowledge of a sequel
that is perpetually hidden in the future and therefore subject to
blind hope. The biographical fact of his Kasrilevkite education in-
sures the further limitation of his knowledge of the great world into
which he is thrown. Mendl's misconception of the world gives way
to double irony when it is filtered through the mind of his wife and
returned to him, transformed again, in the next letter.
 Menakhem-Mendl is a familiar type of comic figure, the innocent cast into the great world where he immediately but only partially absorbs its ways and its language. He relays this new informa-

tion to his wife who throws it back in his face transformed by her own combination of shrewd criticism and innocence. Mendl announces that he has become *a shrayber*; to her he is a *rayber*; he describes the process that will make his fortune in the money market as *stalazhen*, a concept that neither he nor the reader can ever thoroughly grasp but which apparently means that he will buy foreign currency cheap and sell it dear after this "stallage." For his wife *stalazhen* become *delezhansen*, and he patiently explains her mistake:

Stalazhen iz nit, vi du rufst es, delezhansen. Delezhansen iz dos, vos me' fort oif dem keyn Radomishl un keyn Zhitomir.

Stallages are not, as you call them, diligences. Diligences are the things one rides to Radomishl and to Zhitomir.

When Mendl stops dealing with "London" in Odessa—that is, speculating on the difference between the ruble and the English pound—and moves to Yehupetz where he deals in "papers"—that is, speculates on the stock exchange—and then decides to become a broker, Sheyne-Sheyndl recalls for him his failures "mit London, mit di papierlikh—papers—mit di pipernotes." This last, an outgrowth of *papierlekh* grafted onto the stocks which he calls *liliputz* comes out meaning "vipers"—"papers and vipers," she gives him.

The imperfect absorption of foreignisms into written or spoken monologue is a further reflection of the amusing smallness of the world familiar to the speaker or writer. For Menakhem-Mendl the little bits of English, French, and German that he meets on the market are all transformed, and what he leaves unchanged comes back to him remade according to the lights of Kasrilevke. His description of Semedeni's Cafe—a real establishment in Kiev, owned by an Italian and frequented by Sholom Aleichem—returns to him as "Simi-Dina's"—"who in the world is she? In our town there used to be a midwife called Sima-Dina, but she passed away long ago." Foreign or otherwise unfamiliar words suffer a similar fate when put at the mercy of the speaker of oral *skaz*. Either they are reduced to nonsense or they are converted into something familiar.

It is Sheyne-Sheyndl's innocence and invective that combine to remake the world according to her own lights, and it is the medium of written *skaz* that allows Sholom Aleichem to exploit the irony of this transformed speech act. One person addresses another without the intervention of the greater intelligence conventionally associated with a narrator. The innocence of the husband and wife locked in garbled communication is generally amusing and benign. It is just as well that they do not quite understand the full extent of the depravity of the cities. Elsewhere their limitations are more serious and, from the point of view of history, more exasperating. People can be made conscious of their time and place without the benefit of hindsight or travel. The unconsciousness of Menakhem-Mendl and Sheyne-Sheyndl is a source of comedy but it is also a serious limitation that they share with all of Sholom Aleichem's "kleyneh menshelekh mit kleyneh h'shages" (little people with little ideas).

For more than a decade after 1894 the Dreyfus Affair shook the French Republic and drew the attention of the world. Among Jews the accusation of Dreyfus and the public response that first brought the slogan "Death to the Jews" onto the streets of modern Europe had a profound effect. "I was transformed into a Zionist by the Dreyfus Affair," Theodor Herzl recalled shortly before his death in 1904.[14] When he began to organize the settlement of a Jewish state from the diaspora, Herzl, a Viennese journalist working in Paris, knew very little about the Jewish population of Russia and Poland, and he knew nothing of earlier attempts to develop the Zionist idea. Soon eastern Europe would know the case of Dreyfus and the ideas of Herzl well. The way these events and ideas filtered down to the likes of Menakhem-Mendl and his "wise and modest helpmeet" became a source of comedy for Sholom Aleichem. At the same time Kasrilevkite intransigence became a subject of wry satire.

Dreyfus is the subject of a joke told, but not entirely understood, by Sheyne-Sheyndl. Like most digressions from the main events of their lives, the exchange on the subject of Dreyfus is carried out in postscripts. First Sheyne-Sheyndl tells her husband the story of the local "mademoiselle" who has rejected every suitor until she is finally brought one that seems to her liking. The young people are left alone:

Says the bride to the fiancé, "What are they saying about Dreyfus in your town?" Says he, "Which Dreyfus?" Says she to him, "You don't know which Dreyfus?" Says he, "No, what does he deal in? . . ." So she burst out of the room and faints, and the poor fiancé has to return to his town in disgrace. . . .

And by the way, since you are among people of the world, will you please explain to me who is this Dreyfus, and why is the whole world making such a fuss over him?

One would think that the telling of this little story would require that the teller understand the allusion. But Paris is outside the boundaries of Sheyne-Sheyndl's world. She knows just enough to know that Dreyfus is not a local businessman. Beyond that she refers to her worldly husband in Yehupetz. Menakhem-Mendl's clarification of the case makes it even more complicated than it really was, if that is possible. To the intrinsic difficulties of the facts Menakhem-Mendl adds the twists and turns of uncorrected speech that are associated with *skaz* as a form:

> This is how it goes. It seems that in Paris there was a Captain Dreyfus; that is, a captain who was called Dreyfus. There was also Esterhazy who was a major. (A major is bigger than a captain, or maybe it's the other way around—a captain is bigger than a major.) Anyhow, he was a Jew— Dreyfus, I mean. And Esterhazy, the major, was not a Jew. So he went and wrote a *bordereau*.

He follows the story through the comings and goings of Zola and the generals and the lawyers until it begins to sound very much like one of his own business deals. Finally "he was judged guilty and not guilty—make of that what you will. . . . Is the story of Dreyfus quite clear to you now?"

Sheyne-Sheyndl responds from Kasrilevke with questions which are really quite reasonable if we consider the clarity of the report and the narrowness of the world in which she lives. "How can a Jew become a captain?" she asks, since in the Russian Army promotion was impossible for a Jew. "And what is that *bondero* which they keep tossing from one to another?" The event itself diminishes into trivia and is never fully understood. Sholom Aleichem would repeat the ironic reception of "Dreyfus in Kasrilevke" in a story of that name written two years later (1902) and collected under the heading "Little People with Little Ideas."[15] Kasrilevke receives news of the world through Zeydl, the one man in town who subscribes to a newspaper. The first response to the arrest is simple: "What won't a Jew do to make a living?" But when they discover that Dreyfus was falsely accused and when the case is reopened, Kasrilevke rises to the occasion. How then do "little people" assimilate the news of the world? By translating it into local and domestic terms:

> "Ah, I would have liked to have been there when he met his wife."
> "And I would have liked to see the children when they were told, 'Your father has arrived.' "

When Zeydl is forced to report the ambiguous verdict—guilty and not guilty—his townsmen do not blame the judges or the generals or the French people but Zeydl himself, because he is closest at hand. They do not believe him.

Zionism meets the same skeptical reception in Kasrilevke. It must be remembered that this cycle of Menakhem-Mendl letters was written only two years after the first Zionist Congress at Basel in 1897. The movement was not new, but the international organization was. The impact was immense and immediate throughout eastern Europe. Sholom Aleichem was already contributing stories to the Zionist journal *Der Yid,* and he later attended several of the International Congresses. The new movement enters the letters through the limited vision of the protagonists. Sheyne-Sheyndl asks Mendl for more information: "They say that in Yehupetz people are getting registered for the Holy Land. Anybody who pays a deposit for forty kopeks will go. . . ." Presumably the forty kopeks represents a donation rather than a registration, but put in Sheyne-Sheyndl's way it sounds like the kind of lunatic scheme that might engage her husband who nonetheless recognizes that she is describing Zionism. "This is a very noble idea, even though they don't seem to think much of it on the Yehupetz exchange." He would prefer that the Zionists spoke Yiddish and not Russian at their meetings. This Zionist tendency to abjure the use of the language of the Exile often alienated Yiddishists, and Mendl's position may reflect Sholom Aleichem's early uncertainty. But on the whole it is clear that the unspoken authorial sympathy rests with the new movement. Mendl admits that he has raised the subject with several companions at the exchange. They scoff. "Zionism! Doctor Herzl! What kind of business is that!"

America, no doubt, would be more to their liking, the land where business was known to thrive and whither one by one businessmen disappear. When we last hear from Menakhem-Mendl he too is going to America:

Why America all of a sudden? Because they say that in America life is good for Jews. They say that gold is rolling in the streets, yours for the picking. Their money is reckoned in dollars, and people—people are held above rubies. . . . Everybody assures me that in America I'll make good, please God—and they mean *good*. Everyone is going to America these days because there is nothing to do here. Absolutely nothing. All business is finished. Well, if everybody is going why shouldn't I go, too? What have I got to lose?

This is Mendl's last flight, and we are left to assume the usual conclusion. The American dream is for Sholom Aleichem the last fantasy of the Jewish *luftmensh. A boydem,* he would say, an empty attic, dreams returned to dust.

Irony in Sholom Aleichem begins as an attitude toward language. The choice to hold the spoken language up for inspection as something worthy of special attention already implies the distance required by irony. Sholom Aleichem appeals to an audience that recognizes popular locution and is amused by it in a way that people who are completely bound within the style of life and speech are not. Sholom Aleichem wrote for a society that was already uprooted, no longer living in the villages, rarely in the small towns, but mostly in big cities both within the Pale and beyond, in Warsaw and in America. Millions of his readers had been born in the world that he describes; most had left it, and it itself had changed. We look to his novels and his plays for a record of that change. In drama and long narration Sholom Aleichem steps out of the world in which he writes, the small world bound by the range of one voice speaking.

CHAPTER 5

Novelist and Playwright

SHOLOM Aleichem was the master of short monologues and sketches of life in the Russian Pale. He was able to extend these into sequences that center around a person or a place. Stories about Tevye, Menakhem-Mendl, Mottel, or about Kasrilevke have all been collected in separate volumes where they form a sufficiently coherent whole to be read together. But mastery of the monologue and sketch does not lead to mastery of long narration nor, in the case of Sholom Aleichem, did it lead to success in the seemingly compatible art of drama. Sholom Aleichem's initial failure as a playwright tells us more about the state of the Yiddish theater in his time than it does about his capacity for adapting dialogue to the stage. His weakness as a novelist is largely a weakness of form, but what he says in the novels will tell us a great deal about the state of the arts, especially theatrical art, in his time.

I   The Novels

Aside from several notable exceptions it is probably true that the story and the novel are not compatible forms. Boris Eixenbaum describes the difference in his essay on O. Henry: "The difference is one of essence, a difference in principle, conditioned by the fundamental distinction between big and small form. Not only individual writers but also individual literatures cultivate either the novel or the short story." Up to a point Eixenbaum's general distinctions seem to cover the case of Sholom Aleichem. "The novel," he says, "derives from history, from travels; the story, from fairy tale, anecdote." But as he continues it becomes clear that in favoring the examples of Poe and O. Henry he is not describing the kind of story that has thrived in Russia. The short story "amasses its whole weight toward the ending. Like a bomb dropped from an airplane, it must speed downward so as to strike with its warhead full-force on the target. I am speaking here, of course, of the story of action, leaving aside stories of the sketch or *skaz* type, typical, for instance, of Russian literature.''[1] As we have seen *skaz* moves toward its conclusion in a crablike manner progressing through movement from side to side. If it does not transfer into the novel it is not for the same reasons that govern the forms practiced by Poe and O. Henry. The speaker defeats rapid motion toward an end through an endless capacity for digression. Sholom Aleichem exercises delicate control over the wandering of his speakers as they move back and forth. What suits the verbal flow of the speaking voice so well cannot be sustained by a third-person narrator over the course of several hundred pages. In the stories digression emanates from the single point of view of a character whose verbal wanderings are our main interest. The novels wander without the certainty that there is a fixed center of consciousness. For long stretches it is difficult to say who is at the center of the novels, and a reader may get the impression that the author himself is not entirely in control of the dispersion of interest. The early novel *Stempenyu* is a typical example.[2] After introducing Stempenyu the fiddler in the first chapter, Sholom Aleichem leaves the titular hero and gives half the book to the "biography" of Rachel, the woman he loves. The return to Stempenyu in chapter 14 is accomplished with an unconvincing formula: "Let us leave the Queen's daughter and return to the King's son. We shall leave Rachel and speak of Stempenyu." Then we learn what is to be known of the hero's family, his youth, the nature of the musical milieu, and finally his marriage to Freidl, which has taken place before the narrative begins. Only then can we advance to the denouement. Aside from the few meetings of the hero and heroine, principals from the two sides of the story come together only once in a comic interlude when Rachel has encouraged her mother-in-law to go and buy a necklace from Freidl so that she can deliver a message to Freidl's husband. The action of the novel boils down to the events of a few chapters. The rest is given to the description and analysis of Jewish life in the Pale.

When Sholom Aleichem set out to reform Yiddish fiction in the 1880s it was the content rather than the form that caught his attention. He was especially displeased with the sentimental romances of N. M. Shaykevitsh. Ruth Wisse explains his complaint:

The convention of the sentimental romance . . . was inappropriate to serious Jewish literature, he argued, because Jewish life had no use for the ideals of romantic love which had inspired Christian Europe since the Middle Ages. For traditional Jews, love was the result of marriage and not vice versa, and an author was being false to the facts if he portrayed *shtetl* characters driven by passion to commit adultery and/or suicide.[3]

Since the novel was so closely identified with the conventions of romantic love Sholom Aleichem was compelled to make his detachment from his detested predecessors quite explicit. An early novel, *Sender Blank,* is called "A roman ohn a roman," a novel without romance. It is the story of greed and paternal tyranny in a middle-class family, a subject to which he would return in later plays and novels. His next novels, *Stempenyu* and *Yosele Solovey,* both describe the failure of romantic love among Jews in the small towns of the Pale. Mendele, the grandfather, shared Sholom Aleichem's understanding of this subject to the extent that in a letter quoted in the introduction to *Stempenyu* he advises the young writer to avoid the *roman* altogether. "Your genre is elsewhere," he writes, "If there are romances in the lives of our people they are quite different from those of other peoples. One must understand this well and write quite differently." Sholom Aleichem assures Mendele that his *Yidisher Roman,* as he calls *Stempenyu,* is based on his own thorough knowledge of Jewish customs and characters, not on notions borrowed from romances. *Stempenyu* and *Yosele Solovey* both appeared in the *Yidishe Folksbiblyotek,* and both take their place as part of the critical manifesto that was to be exemplified by works published in the new journal. Both novels include attacks on the sentimental romances and the effect that they had on Jewish life. We are told that the virtuous young woman, Rachel, in *Stempenyu* never reads romances. When Esther and Yosele quietly acknowledge their attachment in *Yosele Solovey* we are assured that "neither of them had ever read romances." These silent vows do not bind Yosele. He is seduced by Perele *di Dame,* and Sholom Aleichem allows us to associate Perele's evil designs with the books read to her by her maid. "He is as handsome as the morning star," Leah says of Yosele:

"Just like that Solomon of whom they write in the romances—'tall, well-built, fair of hair. . . .' " Leah the Maid loved to read books that described themselves on the front page with the words, "A very interesting

romance. Copying Forbidden!'' She read these books out loud to
Perele. . . . Perele pretended to laugh at these romances, but at the same
time she enjoyed them.[4]

Although Sholom Aleichem set out to improve Jewish life and literature through his critique of the cheap novel he was unable to offer
a fully formed alternative. In his own novels a broad and realistic
picture of Jewish life is impaired by imperfect control of the form.

In *Stempenyu* Sholom Aleichem shows the strength of the forces
that militate against sentimental romance in the Jewish towns.
Stempenyu is a traveling violinist who plays at fairs and weddings.
He is the stuff romances are made of, a beautiful troubador without scruple in love. One of his liaisons backfires and he finds himself married to Freidl, a shrewish businesswoman who does what
she can to restrain his temperament, his amorous adventures, and
his art. Rachel, ''the Queen's daughter,'' is bound by an equally
unsatisfactory marriage. This beautiful and ardent young woman
has been married off to a shallow young man who is allowed by his
rich parents to spend his days in desultory study of Talmud. His
mother protects her daughter-in-law to the extent that she is completely insulated from the world to which she is drawn. At a
friend's wedding she meets the fiddler, Stempenyu, who sets out to
seduce her. Eventually she consents to join him one evening at the
monastery wall. The presence of the monastery suggests that the
liaison represents as severe a deviation from virtue as conversion,
and Rachel is the most virtuous of Jewish daughters. Already in the
arms of her possible lover, it is the imagined apparition of a friend
who died for love that forces her to draw back, murmur the dead
woman's name, and flee. All Stempenyu sees in the dusk are the
flying ends of her white shawl, ''like the wings of a flying angel.''
Rachel's virtue is rewarded. She returns to the home where she has
been coddled and protected and separated from her husband and
encourages him, in private, to admit his love. Apparently Stempenyu has awakened these needs in her, and she redirects them in a
sanctioned way. At the same time she is able to convince her
Moyshe-Mendl that they should leave his family and go to
Yehupetz and establish a life of their own. They do, and we are told
that a year later they have a successful business and a child. In a last
chapter we see Stempenyu as Samson, shorn of all his powers by
Freidl, the Delilah to whom he is bound. He is consoled only by his
veltel, his little world of music and musicians.

Stempenyu is made to suffer because of his sexual excursions; Rachel is rewarded for her ability to resist. And yet this apparent celebration of the "Jewish Daughter" cannot be made to support all of the traditions in which she is raised. Her "biography" tells the story of a typical woman raised above the level of pauperdom in the *shtetl*. As a child she is sent to *kheder* with her brothers in order to get her out from under foot. Then she is given further lessons by a "girls' teacher." Rachel has always had a sweet singing voice and loves music. If she were not a girl her parents would consider cultivating her talent. As it is, when she is sixteen, her mother tells her it is not proper for a marriageable girl to sing *lieder,* and a husband is found. Her parents "get rid of her," but she is considered lucky because Moyshe-Mendl strikes everyone as a fine bridegroom. His parents are rich. They offer *kest,* food and lodging, to the young couple. Before the wedding the young man writes letters in Hebrew interspersed with German and Russian which she reads with the help of her teacher. They meet once. After the marriage he is less attentive, spending most of his time with his friends in the synagogue while his mother smothers Rachel with kindness. We see her force-fed with sweets through the day. Her life is clearly unpalatable until she meets Stempenyu. His music first and then his good looks attract her, and because she is a virtuous married woman she is allowed to talk with him unguarded by the duenna who would inevitably accompany the unmarried. And yet when she finally resists Stempenyu it is not her virtue nor the attraction of domestic life, but superstitious dread of a dead friend that draws her away. The marriage itself is up to that time without meaning or feeling, and yet Sholom Aleichem is willing to strain our belief by converting the weak husband into a responsible and devoted mate in order to show that the old prearranged marriage can be made to work. As Ruth Wisse has pointed out, the rebellion of Tevye's daughters would present a more clear-cut break with the past.

Yosele Solovey, the story of a cantorial artist, is another "Yidisher Roman" which tests the advances of romance in Jewish life. Here again on either side of a young performer are women who act as foils for each other and alternatives for him. Perele traps and marries him; the virtuous Esther waits at home, forsaken, and is forced to marry an obnoxious older and richer man, Alter Pessie's. Again the novel is split drastically. When Yosele marries Perele we leave him for seven long chapters in which Esther's fate is decided. He is then allowed to return at the moment of her marriage and make one last attempt to draw her away. But now she is a married woman and true to the code and cannot leave her husband however miserable she may be. She languishes, and Yosele goes mad.

Esther's virtue is not to be confused with weakness or with innocence. Her father had taught her to read and write and when he died she had joined her mother in the shop which she helps to manage. Not only in the town of Mazapevke but at the three major fairs in the region she is known as a capable manager of the business. It is she who, as a girl, arranges for Yosele's musical education with Mitzi the cantor in Tetravetz. Esther's capabilities are not unusual in her town. Mazapevke is known for its strong, independent women:

> At a time when people in other parts of the world wrangled over the question of whether a woman could be entrusted with a job, or whether her only concern should be her house, the cooking and children, the Mazapevke Jews stood aside and laughed slyly to themselves. For in Mazapevke from time immemorial the women had been as important as the men. . . . There were men in the town of whom nobody had heard. In many families it was the woman who gave her husband her name instead of the other way around. Zlata the Notions Seller was one of these women, known among Jews as *eyshes-khayel,* a woman of valor. . . . Her husband Levi was called Levi Zlata's, that is, Levi the husband of Zlata.[5]

The independence of these women has a significant limitation: a Woman of Valor had to be married, and she had to bear children. Not to do these things, not to be married, not to have children, is to be an object of pity, not respect. There is no place for her as an unmarried woman. Since she is capable at business, Esther thinks briefly of leaving Mazapevke and working in another town. Here again she is trapped by *yikhus,* by the honor of her family. Could the daughter of Zlata, the granddaughter of Bassya and Reb Avremel Slativer, accept a job from strangers? Betrayed by Yosele, she succumbs to the requirements of her sex and station.

Esther's engagement and wedding are described in gruesome detail. She is likened to the daughter of Jeptha who is sacrificed by her father. Everything about the traditional wedding is made to resemble a sacrifice. Her hair is shorn in preparation for the marriage wig, she begins the fast before the wedding, and then the wedding itself is followed by enforced celebration. Sedate men are made to play the fool *mit gevald,* by force. Yosele's father, Shmulik the Cantor, is heartbroken over the absence and the silence of his son; at the same time his cantorial voice is beginning to crack, and yet he too is forced to rejoice, forced to drink glass after glass of *mashke* until he joins the mad antics of the dancers. Esther's wedding is a phantasmagoria, a dance of death with the pale fainting bride as the death's head.

In these two early novels Jewish women are made to renounce romantic love when it visits them in the guise of the performing artist. It is not surprising that the arts would represent romantic release from the normal constraints imposed from within and without on Jewish life in eastern Europe. Performance would be the way out of the ghetto and the *shtetl* for many then as it has been since. The performer was likely to be attractive; he traveled easily and freely, and he might be idolized while other Jews were insulted, ridiculed, or ignored. At the same time the traveling performer was given low status within the community whose stability he challenged.

These are the characters who habitually populate the novels of Sholom Aleichem. In the early novels Stempenyu is a fiddler and Yosele a traveling cantor; more than twenty years later he wrote *Blondzhende Shtern* (Wandering Stars; translated as *Wandering Star*) primarily about actors on the Yiddish stage. In some ways these seductive, worldly characters are among Sholom Aleichem's most innocent creatures. They are extensions of his free orphans, and up to a point they are allowed to live like those children. Stempenyu and his *kapelie* ("little orchestra") lead lives apparently untouched by the necessities of survival outside the mainstream of life as it was lived by most of their contemporaries:

Jewish musicians—and especially in that day—can be compared to gypsies, a separate folk, with their own jargon and their own customs. They always lived joyously, for them every day was Purim, a holiday. They always made merry, they were a carefree lot, joking, playing pranks, turning the world upside down, talking only of happy things. When a musician came home to his wife he ate the best of everything or got nothing at all . . . but was happy nevertheless. Instead of walking he danced. . . . In a word, the musicians lived in the Garden of Eden. Now in the Garden of Eden who thinks about tomorrow?[6]

This brings the *kasril,* the jolly pauper, to mind, but as we have seen, Sholom Aleichem's paupers are also hounded by the worst trials of life in the Pale. Yosele Solovey, like the tailor Shimmen-Eli, finally goes mad. And Stempenyu, left with the final consolation of his "little world" of musicians with its private language and minor pretensions, is pitiful. Art is as unlikely as love to offer the total release implied by the cheap romances.

In *Wandering Star* Sholom Aleichem returns to the twin themes of art and love and tries to resolve the problems posed by both in a happy ending. The ending, with its return to certain conventions that he had once rejected, is weak. His capacity for dealing with mature love had not expanded; final separation is simply replaced by reconciliation, and a peccant lover is not punished. What has enlarged is his sense of the artistic life, particularly the life of the stage, which was given a special edge of satire after his unsuccessful assault on the Yiddish theater in America. In *Wandering Star* Sholom Aleichem anatomizes the Yiddish theater as it moves across Europe from the small towns of Bessarabia to Vienna and London and finally to New York in a way that sheds light on his own difficulties as a playwright.

Wandering Star may be seen as an attempt to finish the stories of childhood. In the first eleven chapters two adolescents are lured from the constraints of *shtetl* life by the exotic promises of theater people. The story of the boy, Leibel, caught by his father stealing food for the actors and forced to renounce his association with the theater, bears elements of "The Penknife" and "The Fiddle" with the important difference that in this case the boy does not return to the sanctioned way of life. He escapes from home with a sack of money and joins the actors. The novel continues where the story ended. The young girl, Reizel, escapes at the same time, but is taken in another direction. Adolescent vows which generally constitute the extent of Sholom Aleichem's ventures into romantic love, are deferred for thirty chapters till the lovers are reunited at the end of the book when both have become successful artists. The separation of the lovers in the novel is a result of Sholom Aleichem's reluctance or inability to describe mature love.

The novel begins in the small world of small-town youth. Leibel Rapalovich is the son of the rich man in Holeneshti, a small town in Bessarabia near the Russian border. Reizel is the daughter of an impoverished cantor who also keeps a *kheder* which Leibel attends. Reizel's mother, a strict traditionalist, keeps her daughter out of the way of the students:

"A girl," she would say, "has no business with boys. For a girl is a girl and boys are boys. . . ." Leah wouldn't even allow Reizel to sing when the boys were at their studies. And Reizel loved to sing better than anything in the world.

Nonetheless the two young people find themselves beside each other on a bench when the theater comes to town. The lights go out:

The audience drew a long breath, shivered, and was still. Leibel didn't know how it had happened, but all at once Reizel's hand, a warm, soft hand, was clasped in his own. He gave it a light squeeze, as though to say, "Happy?" And she replied with a soft pressure which meant, "Very."[7]

Preadolescent love recalls the first story in the "Song of Songs" sequence where the boy, Shimek, praises his love, Buzie, who like Reizel is also a year or two older than he, with verses from the biblical love song. For Buzie, Shimek contrives the kind of magic tales that young Sholom hears from his friend Shmulik the Orphan in the autobiography.

In *Wandering Star* the lure of the fairy tale is replaced by the theater; the orphans and outsiders who exercise the lure in the stories and in the autobiography are now the actors of Albert Shchupak's troupe. Shchupak's troupe comes to a town that has never seen the theater and establishes itself in Ben Rapalovich's barn. The whole town is delighted with the theater, but for the children it is something more. "It was a return to the legendary Garden of Eden. . . . From the moment the curtain went up, Reizel and Leibel fell under a magic spell, forsaking the earth for a region of spirits and fairies, demons and angels." When the curtain goes down they are plunged back to earth. The barn-theater becomes everything for Leibel that the house of the musician Bezborodke had been for Sholom in "The Fiddle," a place of passion and excitement, the very opposite of home and *kheder:* "he watched the rehearsals; he saw with his own eyes how ordinary people transformed themselves with grease paint, wigs, false beards and moustaches, and motley costumes into devils and demons and angels. Backstage was a new world, a gay, free-and-easy, untrammeled . . . world."[8] Leibel is drawn into the theater by Bernard Holtzman, called Hotzmach, the name traditionally give the Yiddish clown. Hotzmach describes for him his own early attraction to the theater. He was a poor orphan, regularly beaten by a fierce uncle, when the theater came to town. He joined the troupe as a jack-of-all-trades, not an actor. One night after the romantic lead had dropped dead unexpectedly, he was thrust on the stage in a mustache and boots. "We were playing a serious piece, a drama entitled *Dora, or the Rich Beggar, by Shakespeare, Revised and Improved by Albert Shchupak, Producer and Director.*" It was a serious piece but at the sight of young Hotzmach the audience laughed. After that he was a regular in the comic business, pasting on earlocks and a tattered gaberdine, singing the song of the little hasid. Hotzmach's life becomes part of the "folklore of the theater" for Leibel, and it is Hotzmach who encourages him first to steal food and cigarettes and then money to leave home and become an actor.

Reizel undergoes similar temptation and conflict. Her parents, like Leibel's, reject the slightest association with theatrical people. An associate of Shchupak's hears her sing the famous lullaby "Rozhinkes mit Mandlen" ("Raisins and Almonds"), which she had heard at the theater. He immediately recognizes a singer's voice and returns with Shchupak himself, who suggests to the cantor that his daughter go on stage. "May my enemies not live to see the day," the cantor's wife screams. "What do you take us for, common trash, cobblers or pants-patchers, to allow our own flesh and blood to join a gang of comedians, acrobats, clowns, vagabonds?" The cantor's wife recognizes that there is a kind of singing that is approved by the community and a kind that is not. In *Yosele Solovey* and later in *Wandering Star* with the entry of the Lomzsha cantor who goes on stage as the Lomzsha Nightingale, Sholom Aleichem traces the thin line that divides religious practice from popular performance. The Yiddish theater would shamelessly draw on religious songs and themes as well as on the personnel of the synagogue as it advanced in popularity. But now in Holeneshti the line is drawn for Reizel, and she cannot accept it. "Silently she decried the fate which had consigned her to these dismal surroundings, to narrow, bigoted people who shut out the big world without ever having tasted its joys."

On the same night Leibel and Reizel escape. They are taken in separate carriages in separate directions by Hotzmach and Shchupak whose theatrical collaboration thus ends. Before they part and before Shchupak's conspiracy draws them apart, the two meet and make their mutual vows. The scene of the two young lovers together on the night of the great fire in God's Street can be compared with the similar scene which precedes the separation of Yosele Solovey and Esther. In both cases the vows culminate an adolescent romance. In the later novel the young woman is allowed to share the young man's dreams. She too plans to advance in her art. The fact that the woman is allowed to share the rejection of *shtetl* life and the expectation of release is the result of social changes during the crucial quarter century between the early and the late novels. As we have seen, Tevye's daughters are also born of these changes. During the night of the fire in God's Street Leibel recognizes their shared fate:

The fate which had condemned them both to the brutishness and vulgarity of life in Holeneshti had also miraculously thrown them together and awakened the same longings in both of them. Now it was working for their deliverance. Together they would burst the bonds; together they would set out into the wide world to begin a new life, a happy, free, joyous life. They would tread the same path, share the same studies, follow the same muse . . . and some day become famous together, he as an actor, she as a singer.

The flame in the street diminishes and the sky darkens and Reizel points to the falling stars. "It's natural for them to fall," Leibel explains. "Stars always seem to be falling. But they don't really fall; they wander." Leibel momentarily assumes the role of "an older and wiser brother" and explains "the mystery of the stars. Each [is] the soul of a human being. Wherever a man's star wandered, he had to follow. That [is] why the stars always seem to be falling. Stars do not fall; stars wander."[9] The stars represent their separate fates, their ideals, and, in the theatrical sense, stars are also actors who like Jews are obliged to wander.

With the escape of Leibel and Reizel the childhood fantasy ends. These childish fantasies that are generally repressed or allowed to wither in other stories are extended beyond the *shtetl* into the great world in the novel. Before this the major difference between these first eleven chapters of *Wandering Star* and the stories of childhood is that the novel is narrated in the third person. "The Penknife," "The Fiddle," and "The Page from the Song of Songs" are told in the first person. Although the stories are told from the distance implied by retrospect, the first person conveys the impression that we

are caught within the boundaries of a single child's mind. The
novel seeks to go beyond that, first into the separate though parallel experiences of two children, and then out into the great world
where more space and time and many more characters are to be exposed along with the institution of the Yiddish theater. We lose
both the intimacy and the irony of the stories. We gain a certain
breadth of theme illustrated by an abundance of comic characters
who advance the satire of the theatrical world.

Wandering Star, like *Shomers Mishpet,* is the satire of an art. In
Sholom Aleichem's critique of the Yiddish theater it is the patrons,
the public, and the actors rather than the writers who bear the
brunt of the satire. During the course of the novel we follow the
Yiddish theater from its roots among Purim players and *kheder*
boys to the small towns of Rumania, Bukovina, and Bessarabia
where troupes of actors traveled from town to town. Eventually
these same performers were lured "uptown" into the English-lan-
guage theaters of New York. This historical evolution represented
by the course of events in the novel is really very short. In 1876
Abraham Goldfaden encouraged Jewish singers in Jassy, Rumania,
to perform a play around their songs; by the 1920s it was common
for actors like Muni Weissenfreund to turn about and become Paul
Muni, an American actor. It is a Goldfaden song—"Rozshenkes
mit Mandlen"—that Shchupak's partner, Sholom Meyer Muravchik, first hears Reizel sing. When Leibel Rapalovich is taken from
his home in Bessarabia he is given the name of Leo Rapelesco both
to camouflage his escape and to create the impression that he comes
from Rumania, the source of Yiddish theater. Jassy is one of the
towns visited by the performers.

In Sholom Aleichem's panorama of the Yiddish theater it is the
entrepreneur who is subjected to the harshest criticism. He also has
harsh words for the professed "lovers of the Yiddish theater" like
Dr. Levias, or Leviathan, as he is called by the actors in Lemberg.
Levias praises the actors and puffs himself at their expense and
never parts with any money on their behalf. The actual promoters
come under more fire. They recur in different garb from the
Bessarabian villages to New York, but the more we penetrate the
new world the more we are likely to look upon the original villains
with affection. Shchupak and Muravchik moving in on Holeneshti
are fairly innocent marauders next to Mr. Nickel, the full-scale
capitalist in New York. As long as they are operating in the small
towns of eastern Europe the petty promoters rouse the same com-

bination af amusement and discomfort that we sense in the adventures of the Duke and the King in *Huckleberry Finn* or Vincent Crummles in *Nicholas Nickleby.*

Whether in Holeneshti or in New York the methods are largely the same. Outrageous advertisement precedes the equally outrageous performance of musical-comical-tragical extravaganzas. The theater as we meet it in *Wandering Star* relies mostly on false advertisement. That Leibel Rapalovich turns out to be an excellent actor has little to do with his initial appeal as Leo Rapelesco of Bucharest who is said to have performed for the delight of the King of Rumania. In Lemberg, Getzel ben Getzel promotes Yentel Schwalb as Henrietta Schwalb, the well-known singer and actress from Buenos Aires. Later Yentel's brother Nissel will create the "Lomzsha Nightingale" out of the starving cantor from Lomzsha: "Come This Day to our theater to hear the Lomzsha Nightingale sing Kol Nidre with his own choir which won the acclaim of King George of England."[10] The chicanery of Shchupak, Getzel ben Getzel, and their type is all mitigated by a certain charm that is withheld from their more thoroughly Anglicized or Americanized counterparts, Mr. Klammer and Mr. Nickel. Nissel Schwalb proves that he can operate in both worlds. Klammer is a restaurateur hungry for power. He is drawn into the theater business by Nissel Schwalb who had earlier seen to it that London's major Yiddish theater fell into the hands of a cold Englishman named Hotchkiss. Klammer joins Nissel Schwalb to form a company that will take Rapalesco to America. There they are in turn promoted by Mr. Nickel at whose theater Rapalesco makes his American debut. Nickel is an amiable man, a "good guy," and the king of "bluffers." Bluff, according to Sholom Aleichem, is a word of American origin:

To bluff is not to tell an outright lie or fib, it is not to babble or rant, to spin yarns out of thin air. . . . An American is too much of a businessman for that. When an American tilts his head to one side, tucks his thumb in his vest, and tells you a lie, it is rounded out, just plausible enough to be believed, certainly hard to refuse, and above all, it sticks to the business at hand.[11]

Nickel and his colleagues are absorbed in bluffing each other and then in bluffing the public. and these are the people who control the theater. The public form taken by bluff is advertisement, and we learn that the Yiddish theater in America rises and falls on the success of its advertisement. This, of course, is not a Jewish invention. In the nineteenth century such masters of bluff and puffery as P. T. Barnum fixed the kinship of entertainment and advertisement. The result in the Yiddish theater as it is described by Sholom Aleichem sounds very much like a Barnum production. What succeeds in New York is a "colossal musical-dramatic-national-patriotic-tragicomedy called *Moishe.*"

In the Yiddish theater extravaganzas like *Moishe* were called *shund* ("trash"). Sholom Aleichem describes two alternatives to *shund* in *Wandering Star.* The first is the rough and ready traveling productions of eastern Europe. This was not "art" to be sure, but it was high-spirited, passionate acting and singing by untrained, unestablished performers who were obliged to make the most of very little. This is the theater of Hotzmach, the clown, Rapalesco's first mentor. Hotzmach takes his protégé as far as London where he is halted by the tubercular cough that kills him. It is clear that he cannot go to America, that he must remain in Europe. He emanates from the folk. He is another of Sholom Aleichem's orphans, a creature from the fringe of society, a natural as a comedian, and he is such a natural pauper that he cannot be converted to anything else. As a successful theater director in a top hat and necktie he remains a comic character. We recognize in him one of the marked figures into whom the middle-class author pours himself. It is notable that he shares Sholom Aleichem's medical symptoms and receives the same medical advice—winters in Italy, summers in Switzerland. Sholom Aleichem followed the advice and was recovering though still coughing while he wrote *Wandering Star.* Hotzmach could not possibly follow such prudent advice and dies in London, a city found repugnant by both author and character. Hotzmach, unlike Sholom Aleichem, never was forced to make the final adaptation to America.

Even before London, Hotzmach's theater had begun another change. A prompter whom he had picked up along with Yentel Schwalb in Lemberg, one Benny Gorgel, a "man of education," had stumbled upon a Yiddish translation of Karl Gutzkow's *Uriel Acosta.* However ponderous Gutzkow's play may seem now, the tale of an excommunicated Jewish heretic who commits suicide with his lover was bound to grip certain Jewish audiences at the turn of the century. Young renegade hasidim in Czernowitz were overwhelmed by it. In New York not everyone was sure what to make of the play, "not everyone knew who the author was—Lateiner or Gordon or Lubin or Professor Jacobi. Some waited for a 'plot' to develop and maybe a song or two. Which demonstrates how highly developed the taste of the public was. . . ." The addition of such a play to the expected repertoire (indicated by the names of the expected authors) is as surprising as Rapalesco's style of acting, "without ranting or posturing, no clutching at the heart, no tearing of hair, no wringing of hands, no striding up and down the stage, no contortion of features." [12]

In Europe neither the new theater nor the new style of acting had made much sense to Hotzmach. Rapalesco spoke to him of "the wide world . . . and the open sky" of the Yiddish theater: "That 'wide world and open sky' were Greek to Holtzman, along with the prattle about 'self-expression,' a 'reformed theater,' a 'new repertory,' everything new, new, new. And what, Holtzman asked himself, would become of the old?" [13]

In *Wandering Star* Sholom Aleichem does not make it clear what direction the Yiddish theater will take. Leibel is reunited with Reizel; that is, Rapalesco is reunited with Rosa Spivak, who has left the Yiddish stage and become a noted international singer. The novel concludes in a series of inconclusive letters written by several principals. Rosa writes of her husband that "his ideal is the stage and his goal is to reform the Yiddish theater and place it on as high a plane as possible," but we are told little of how that is to be done besides the fact that the husband and wife return to Europe. In effect, the question is left where it would remain for the next thirty years—art or *shund*?

The Yiddish theater becomes a character in *Wandering Star*, a character whose future engages our imagination in a way that the future of few of the human characters can. Rapalesco and Rosa Spivak are allowed to fade out when their reunification is assured. The fate of minor characters is closely linked with the fate of the theater. Isaac Schwalb, younger brother of Nissel, began as a bombastic Purim player, joined the Lemberg theater with his sister Yentel, and became fairly competent in the heavy roles. In New York he works in the high galleries of Nickel's theater as a claquer, artificially drumming up support in the audience. Thus the career of this minor character reflects the progress of the Yiddish stage from Purim players to wandering actors to American advertisers. On the whole it is the wealth of minor characters who support the comedy in all of the novels. They reveal themselves in little bits of dialogue and in little vignettes that Sholom Aleichem had mastered in the writing of short stories. On board the ship to America in *Wandering Star* the clean-shaven ex-cantor of Lomzsha suddenly appears on deck in his Sabbath gaberdine with a silken sash and a pious face. His theatrical friends ask for an explanation:

> "America," answered the cantor curtly. But since the one word didn't seem to satisfy his audience, he went on to enlighten them. "America, you understand, is not Europe, and New York is not London. America is a land of 'either-or.' Either you're one thing or you're another. If you're an artist, you're an artist. If you're a cantor, you're a cantor. Take that between your teeth and chew it."[14]

The cantor who barely speaks another line in the book tells the whole story of his marginal position between respectable religious observance and undignified performance from which he contrives his false and fragile dignity according to a misconception of life in America. Not long afterward, he finds himself singing *"Kol Nidre* every night in the famous operetta called, by strange coincidence, *Kol Nidre,"* a musical named for the famous prayer chanted on the eve of Yom Kuppur. The cantor performs with his whole family, each of whom plays a different instrument like the family of Bezborodke in "The Fiddle."

Wandering Star is filled with amusing theatrical types. Less impressive are the undeveloped characters of the major figures. Long narration does not bring Sholom Aleichem as close to these major characters as the short monologues and dialogues that are implanted in the novels and that comprise the best of his short stories. The hero and heroine sometimes diminish in interest, because with the exception of Stempenyu and his musician's jargon they are forbidden the amusing features of speech and tics of behavior that identify the others. In other respects the long fiction falters in the attempt to tell two parallel stories. Transitions are awkward and artificial. Flashbacks are required to catch up for lost time in the companion plot, thus putting time quite out of joint. Although the themes of love and art are more thoroughly integrated in *Wandering Star* than in the earlier novels, their linkage is sometimes fortuitous. Does Rapalesco go to Vienna and then London and New York because he hears that Rosa has preceded him in each of these places or because they happen to be the centers of his professional life as an actor? Conveniently Rosa shares his theatrical ambitions so love and art are allowed to advance together. He follows her star.

The strength of *Wandering Star* does not lie in the ingenuity of its structure nor in the creation of its major characters but rather in its portrayal of the entire Yiddish theater in midstream. This was the theater that first drew Sholom Aleichem to America in 1906. At first he was greatly puffed by the newspapers, but when two of his plays opened at the same time in February, 1907, both closed within two weeks. He returned to Europe dejected, and especially discouraged with America and its Yiddish theater. We have said that in his satire of the theater Sholom Aleichem aimed primarily at the entrepreneurs and journalists and "lovers of the Yiddish stage." These and their companion public had been his stumbling block. Little is said of writers largely because the Yiddish theater was not yet a writer's theater. It was dominated by the great actor-directors and managers such as Thomashefsky and Adler, who took whatever liberties they wished with scripts.[15] Sholom Aleichem's real success on stage would only follow various reforms in the Yiddish theater, perhaps of the kind anticipated by Rapalesco.

II *The plays*

The Yiddish critic Alexander Mukdoyni has said that Sholom Aleichem was essentially a dramatist who turned to writing fiction because in his time producers and theaters were hard to find, while Yiddish newspapers and journals were plentiful and accepted his work eagerly. Mukdoyni cites Sholom Aleichem's skill in the writing of dialogue and in the creation of dramatic situations as well as the ease with which his novels and stories were later adapted to the stage as proof of his contention. The failure of his plays to find acceptance during his lifetime is ascribed to the immaturity of the Yiddish stage, which was still laboring under the handicap of *shund* theater, the subject of his own satire in *Wandering Star.*[16]

In Russia itself where the Yiddish theater was banned after 1883 there was certainly no encouragement for the playwright. The Yiddish theater enjoyed a marginal existence in the borderlands, and further west in Rumania and Galicia under the less inhibiting government of the Austro-Hungarian empire. Further west in America the Yiddish theater would thrive under the spell of Adler and Thomashefsky, but the making of a genuine art theater did not come about until after Sholom Aleichem's death. Immediately after the war Maurice Schwartz and Jacob Ben Ami, together and in separate ventures, initiated the Yiddish Art Theater in New York, where the plays of Peretz Hirshbein and Sholom Aleichem were to be seen along with those of Chekhov, Shaw, and Gorki. In May, 1919, Schwartz produced Sholom Aleichem's *Menshen (People),* in August of that year the author's dramatization of *Tevye,* in 1920 *Shver tsu zayn a yid (It's Hard to be a Jew),* and two years later *Dos Groyse Gevins (The Great Winning).* At the end of the decade he added dramatizations of *Stempenyu* and *Wandering Star.* Another company, the Folksbiene, produced *It's Hard to be a Jew* as well as a number of one-act plays adapted from stories in the 1920s and 1930s. After 1928 Artef—the Arbeiter Teater Farband—produced a number of plays, most successfully *Dos Groyse Gevins* under the title of *200,000* in 1936-37. In both production and politics Artef was influenced by the rise of a Yiddish theater in the Soviet Union. Immediately after the Revolution Alexander Granovsky initiated what would become the Jewish State Theater in Moscow, a forum both for dramatic experiment and political interpretation of Yiddish plays, including those of Sholom Aleichem.

As long as Sholom Aleichem actually lived in Russia as a writer there was no established Yiddish theater. The ban that began in 1883 when his first Yiddish stories appeared was lifted in 1908 when he was living abroad. His career as a playwright began in the turmoil of 1905 that hastened his departure, and his most notable plays all reflect the social unrest of that particular period. His first play, *Tsuzeyt un Tsushpreyt (Scattered and Dispersed)* was performed in the spring of 1905 in Warsaw in a Russian translation.[17] For this initiation of a dramatic career we may adapt Mukdoyni's analysis: if newspapers were to profit from his essentially dramatic gift, his drama for its part would always bear the immediacy of journalism. *Scattered and Dispersed* was written as a feuilleton for the *Yidishe Folkszeytung.* The first theater audience loved the play and mobbed the playwright who sat in the theater, delighted and somewhat perplexed by his initial success. Surely the immediate topicality of the play as well as his own popularity as a writer of fiction contributed to the response.

When the play first appeared as a newspaper serial, little attention was given to the exigencies of stage production. It is fragmented into far too many scenes and the attention of the audience is dissipated by far too many actors. The power of the play does not lie in its fitness for the stage but rather in its capacity to give life and language to the great movements that were changing the world of eastern European Jewry throughout the period. The play centers around the family of Meyer Shalant which has recently moved from a *shtetl* to the city. In order to complete the transformation which would have been so familiar to the original audience, Meyer has changed his surname from Tsholent, the Yiddish word for a mixture of barley, beans, scraps of meat and bone, and anything that happens to be on hand, baked overnight for the Sabbath, to the innocuous Shalant. He is a man with a good house, good clothes, and a job as agent for a Polish landowner. The introduction of each character is the introduction of a different response to the new life represented most recently by the move to the city. Meyer's eldest daughter Flora is vain and silly, always seen consulting a mirror. She is recently divorced. The youngest daughter Hannah is an intellectual. She has short hair, scorns parental attempts at matchmaking, and wants to go abroad to study. We discover that the oldest son Matvei is a gambler. Chaim is a Zionist, and Volodya a revolutionary. The only apparently stable element in the household is the mother, Malkeh, a simple, pious woman who regrets the move to the city and meets each new crisis by reading her prayerbook. But in the continual crisis of 1905 even this simplicity and piety provokes variable and unpredictable behavior.

Within the play the crises coalesce around the arrival of the police in search of Volodya, who is suspected of having revolutionary pamphlets in his possession. At the same time Flora has eloped with a dentist, "a nobody," according to her father. Matvei has vanished. When Meyer returns from business to find his family in this turmoil and his wife calmly praying, he turns his anger on her:

MEYER: You are a mother. It is your duty to know what your children are doing, where they are.

MALKEH: What kind of mother am I to whom no one listens? All of you laugh at me. You treat me like dirt. You yourself taught the children to despise me.

Self-defense and defense of tradition become a radical position when the usually dutiful wife makes her stand. The family is dissolving.

The children quickly detach themselves from their father's opportunism and their mother's traditionalism and from each other. Chaim disclaims all knowledge or interest in Volodya's activities and presents his own views as a Zionist in the next scene. Meyer mocks his son's fantasies of a homeland in Palestine, and Chaim rejects his father as "the Count's Jew." Hannah announces that she is leaving home to study in Bern. One catastrophe follows another in what mounts to comedy when the youngest son Sasha enters with a dog he has bought on the street. Meyer shouts at the boy to get out with his dog and the boy runs off weeping and threatening to drown himself. Parental authority has become ludicrous.

Just as the play takes this turn toward farce Meyer is called to his senses by a message from the count requiring his presence at the Grand Hotel. In a frenzy Meyer calls for his boots, his coat, his top hat. Dressed in this finery he hesitates at the door, rubs his forehead and asks, "Malkeh, did you say that Volodya is in prison? Where are all the children?" "Tsuzeyt un tsushpreyt," she answers, "oif alleh zibn yaamen," scattered and dispersed over the seven seas. Meyer Shalant sits at the table and weeps and his wife returns to her role as comforter. "Meyer, God be with you, Meyer. . . ."

All of the frustrations of 1905 are concentrated in Meyer Shalant's tears. Conflicting ideologies and crass materialism along with geographic upheaval combine in an assault on whatever certainties there seem to have been. On the small scale, the family crumbles; at large, Jews are flung further into the *goles,* the dispersion so frequently associated with the random scattering of grain implied by the title of the play.

Much of what Sholom Aleichem wrote in the next several years would continue the image of turmoil and change. For the expression of this turmoil he seeks the vitality of both drama and journalism. The short novel *In Shturm (In the Storm,* 1907) is presented as if it were a play.[18] The subtitle, *A Roman in Two Parts,* could almost be "a play in two acts." The action revolves around the fixed point of 13 Vasilchikover Street where three different families live. The events of 1905 from Revolution to Constitution to pogroms and riots are the substance of the novel which, like *Scattered and Dispersed,* offers representatives of every possible position. Various degrees of assimilation, religion, and rebellion are tested in a series of public crises. These events that lurk in the background of the stories fill the foreground of the journalistic feuilletons and plays.

In the Storm and the plays of this period give a great deal of attention to questions of social class. People of three economic orders occupy the house at 13 Vasilchikover—a rich businessman, powerful in the Jewish community; a middle-class, assimilated druggist, and a poor shoemaker whose sons are most conscious of their membership in the working class. One result of the collective suffering in a time of shared stress is a blurring of class lines. The one-act play called *Menshen,* also written in 1907, describes the profound divisions of class that can remain unmended within one household.[19] In this case the *Menshen* or *People* are servants belowstairs in the house of one Madame Gold. The word *mensh* is dense with connotation. First, a *mensh* is a person and *menshen* are people. But a *mensh* is also a person to be distinguished from an animal; that is, a person who behaves—and is allowed to behave—with human dignity. "Zay a mensh," a father adjures his son. "Be a real person, a human being." In this play *menshen* are people who work for others, a condition that may not allow them the dignity of menshen in the second sense.

As the curtain goes up on the richly appointed kitchen the cook is dictating a letter to her sister. The footman Hertz does the writing. She enumerates all the *menshen* in the house. A *mensh* works in the garden, another tends the horses, a third is a personal valet, and so on. All work with their hands except the overseer Daniel, who deals with accounts, paper, and money. Throughout the play we are reminded of their status as workers. The cook is at the stove, the footman brushes clothes, the maids do cleaning. Their hands never stop even when they speak, weep, or laugh. From above Madame Gold shouts orders. Eventually she appears on stage. Her son, the spoiled profligate, Natan Mayseyevich, never appears but his influence is pervasive, like a foul odor.

Lisa the parlormaid is leaving. Her little red trunk is packed. She has been seduced by Natan Mayseyevich. Again we are in the city and times have changed. It had once been a function of the *nogid* in a small town to employ orphans as maids and with employment give them domestic security. They would be married from the house of the employer and given a dowry. This was a *mitzvah,* a good deed, unknown to the new urban wealth exemplified by Madame

Gold and her son. Lisa is in tears not so much for her own plight but for the possible disgrace it might bring on her sister who works in a shop, a step up from domestic service. Panietchka, a former parlormaid who had also been seduced by the young master, has become a prostitute. Now she comes to visit her old friends and chatters gaily about her fine dwelling, her men friends. Rikel the cook says she sounds too "freylikh," too cheerful, and Panietchka breaks down and tells the other *menshen* that, because of her disgrace, her beloved brother has left town. She whispers that he has become "political." As everyone would know, "political" means revolutionary, and we are to understand that this behavior is not shameful but dangerous, to be hidden in a whisper. It is a way to win back lost dignity. *Menshen* can be real *menshen*.

While Lisa prepares to leave, a new maid arrives accompanied by her parents from a small town. She is innocent of urban life and asks why Lisa has been dismissed. Has she been caught stealing? Fishl, the husband of the cook, who has come to visit from the house where he is employed, answers her with advice: "You will save up some money and get married. May God forbid that after you marry you remain a *mensh*. Better to eat once in three days and be your own person." Fishl speaks for the class of servants. "With them—the employers—is a *mensh* worthy of being a *mensh*? We are enslaved by them. We don't know what a Sabbath is or a holiday. We never see a wife, a child." "Foolishness," says Daniel the overseer, looking up from his account books. Daniel, an old bachelor committed to the service of the family upstairs, lords it over the other servants. He is, according to the stage directions, an inch taller when he speaks to them, and he shrinks when he answers Madame Gold. Fishl before he leaves clenches his fist and curses the woman upstairs. Daniel, hearing her call, shrinks and walks upstairs.

When Madame Gold comes down to the kitchen and finds Panietchka talking to the servants she bursts into a rage. How dare this fallen woman visit her *menshen* and pollute the spotless kitchen? Panietchka sweetly asks after Natan Mayseyevich. As she leaves she says that no doubt she will be running into him. After Panietchka has left, the infuriated mistress shouts at Daniel to dismiss all the servants at once. And Daniel, the submissive Daniel, rises to his feet, throws down the account books, scatters the papers and keys at her feet and shouts back, "I have been silent long enough. . . . She says that you—servants—defile her house. We, *menshen*, defile her house! Let us go. What are we? We are the lowest of low. We are *menshen*." He raises his fist and his voice, *"Menshen! Menshen!"* The word is intended to transform itself in its final repetition into an injunction and a rallying cry and a reminder of the potential dignity of the people. This is the closest of Sholom Aleichem's plays to what might be called proletarian drama. Granovsky produced this play in Moscow after the Revolution, and in New York, where it was part of Schwartz' repertoire, Daniel's final cry would have echoed in the sweatshops.

Sholom Aleichem called his last full-length play *The Great Winning,* a *folks-shpiel* ("folk play").²⁰ In several senses it belongs to the folk. It is both a celebration of the common folk, and it is the reworking of a folk motif that enters nearly every culture including the Jewish. This is the story of the poor man made rich by magical or divine intervention and then returned to poverty. Arabian tales of genii, the Grimm tale of "The Fisherman and his Wife," and the Jewish tales associated with Elijah the prophet follow this pattern. One tale of Elijah describes the prophet visiting a pauper with the promise of seven years of wealth to be followed by the same poverty he has known. The pauper has only to choose whether he wants his good fortune to begin now or at another time. He consults his wife who advises him to take the gift now, but unlike the greedy wife of the fisherman in Grimm, this one chooses to distribute the new wealth to the poor, keeping only what is required to sustain life. When Elijah returns the wife says that she will voluntarily give up the wealth if another can be found for it whose trust is worthy. God hears and allows the pair to continue to live with the wealth. Y. L. Peretz recreates this story in the setting of the *shtetl* in his "Zibn guteh yor" ("Seven Good Years"). Generally the beneficiaries are less virtuous, ape the rich to their sorrow, and return to poverty with the lesson that they are better off poor.

The Great Winning is a pauper's dream come true. A poor tailor, Shimele Soroker, wins the grand lottery prize of 200,000 rubles and is allowed to play the role of a rich man. But the pleasure is brief. He loses his money at one blow, and returns to being a poor tailor. The first half of his story brings to mind the dream of the melamed in "If I Were Rothschild" and all the dreams of Tevye. This is the familiar dream of sudden redemption cast in financial terms. Sholom Aleichem borrows the title of the play from the first of the

Tevye stories. The second of those stories, "A Boydem" ("The Bubble Bursts") tells the story of the inevitable fall when Tevye invests his winnings with his kinsman Menakhem-Mendl. All of Menakhem-Mendl's adventures follow the pattern of a great winning and a subsequent loss with the difference that Mendl never holds the money in his hand. It is always a dream.

Shimele Soroker begins not as a desperate pauper but as a tailor who takes pride in his craft and who happens to be poor. He sings at his work and his song extols his craft and his fellow craftsmen: "Sher un Eizen—Amkho" ("Shears and Iron—Our Folk"). But his rent is long overdue and the rent collector threatens to evict him. Tradesmen are dunning him for his debts. Through all his hardship he has held on to one chance of wealth, a worn and rumpled *vigirsher billet,* a lottery ticket, which he has kept for twenty-five years. At the end of the first act the drawing has taken place, and his daughter Beilke comes home with the news that he has won the grand prize, 200,000 rubles.

In the second act Shimele is a rich man in a fine house filled with furniture that looks as though it has been taken out of a display window of a shop. Everything is new including his name. He is Semyon Matayevich and his wife, Eti-Meni, is Ernestina Yefimovna. Only Beilke refuses to change her clothing or her name to match the sudden wealth. A maid and footman, far more haughty than their master, intervene and refuse entry to Shimele's former comrades, his two apprentices, Kopel and Mottel who have come to see Beilke.

Wealth only changes Shimele superficially. He is clearly playing a part that cannot entirely hide his old self. He is generous, he makes no secret of the fact that he is practically illiterate, and he is bored with his new life as it is. All of this makes him an easy mark for two false speculators who come to him with a chance to augment his fortune in the new film industry. Eti-Meni, still the practical wife, is suspicious until she is assured that the contract will allow her own family and her sister—but, she stipulates, not her sister's family—to attend the moving pictures free. Shimele is in such a hurry to conclude the deal that he does not wait for his daughter to come home and write the check but lets the speculator write it, and he signs it.

In the third act Shimele and his wife are guests at the house of their former landlord, Asher Fine, who had tried to evict them earlier. Now the landlord is eager to make a match between his dandified son and the daughter of the newly rich tailor. But Beilke pleads a headache and stays away. It is at this apparent peak of his new glory that Shimele falls. The bank director and his cashier enter and inform him that he has signed away his fortune with the addition of an extra zero on the check. The check was cashed and the two speculators have absconded with all that was left to him. At the same time the footman enters to announce that Beilke has escaped. No doubt Maurice Schwartz, who had produced his own version of *The Merchant of Venice,* would have had an excellent time with the scene of Shimele begging help to recover his daughter. Only Shimele, unlike Shylock, is not worried about his ducats. Humbled by the double loss, he takes off his shiny new cylinder hat, throws into it his gold watch, orders his wife to throw in her pearls and runs around the room of people crying, "Jews, take my last money. Save me, Jews. Help me find my daughter."

The Great Winning, like *The Merchant of Venice,* is a comedy. The last act takes place at a country inn to which Beilke has fled with the two apprentices, Kopel and Mottel. The two young men engage in a comic competition for the maid. It is clear that one of them, Mottel, has a secret understanding with her, and just as the impromptu competition is concluded, Shimele and Eti-Meni enter. The mother is distraught, but Shimele Soroker is jubilant. Their daughter has not committed the much feared betrayal—conversion and marriage to a Gentile—but rather she is allied with a Jew and a tailor. "Sher un Eyzen," he sings again, "Our folk." The play ends with the singing and dancing that goes with a village wedding. The happy resolution is also a return to the *shtetl.*

It is not only the happy ending that makes *The Great Winning* a comedy. Both the winning and the loss border on farce, and the adventures of an innocent stitcher among the rich are also funny. Depending on the tone of production the play can turn to slapstick or to sharp satire. The folktale upon which it is based may be intended as a lesson to poor people, namely, that they are better off poor. In this case it is not Shimele's poverty but the pride in his work and the camaraderie of other tailors that is celebrated, while the obnoxious manners of Asher Fine and his rich friends are ridiculed. Under a variety of titles the play has had a long and varied history. Granovsky produced a musical version called *200,000* in 1925 with political overtones that influenced the successful Artef production in America a decade later. More recently the play was performed as *The Big Winner* in New York (1974). In this mutation the play became a musical again with a narrator appearing between the acts to explain in English what was about to happen. A play that began sixty years earlier by turning folklore into social satire has reverted not so much to folklore as to something folksy and nostalgic, a pleasant memory of a memory.

Menshen and *Dos Groyse Gevins* pose class against class among Jews. *Shver tsu zayn a yid (It's Hard to be a Jew)* returns contemporary conflict to the arena in which the division between Jew and Gentile is paramount.[21] The action of the play unrolls precisely in the time of its writing, just in the wake of the Beilis case in Russia. Beilis had been acquitted in Kiev, but the threat of blood libel[22] was still very much in the air. It is in this charged atmosphere that two students, a Jew and a Gentile, agree to change places for a year. The change of identity is explained in a scene that precedes the first act of the play. The two students, Hershko Shneyerson and Ivan Ivanovich Ivanov, are celebrating their graduation from the gymnasium with other students who look forward to their entry into the university. Only Hershko is gloomy. He explains that as a Jew he cannot expect entry even though he has graduated from the gymnasium with a gold medal. Ivanov still does not understand why his friend should be gloomy on such a night among friends. Hershko explodes. A few friends are not enough:

You seem to think that the whole world is contained in here, in this room. We and our pals, eh? You're forgetting that there is a world outside the [gymnasium], and a big world at that. There are other people beside us. But you seem to know very little about that big world outside, almost nothing. You know nothing of the hell outside. (pause) If you were in my skin for at least one year, then you'd know, and then you'd feel what it means to be subject to percentages in college, ministerial circulars and similar good things.

Ivanov takes this as an invitation to change identity, and the play that follows is his lesson in the way of the world.

The action of the play occurs in the university town at the home of David Shapiro, where Ivanov goes in the guise of his Jewish friend to find lodging. Shapiro has recently fallen to a minor position in the bourse, though he still likes to show that he knows how to manipulate officials, and he likes to remind his listeners of the original dignity of his family—"the true Shapiros, those from Slavita, you must have heard about them." His wife Sarah rents the room to the newly Judaized Ivanov for whom the deal is made all the more attractive by Shapiro's daughter, Berta Davidovna, a gymnasia student about to graduate. There is also a young son, Syomka, who is constantly being told to attend to his studies. This, then, is a typical Jewish middle-class family, proud of a strictly Jewish tradition, at the same time ready to advance through Russian schools and universities. Hearing the name Shneyerson, Shapiro asks if his lodger belongs to the famous Hasidic family of Lubavich. The young man does not contradict him, and the family marvels that the scion of such a family should not only look like a *goy* but know so little about Jewish life and be unable to speak the *mameh loshen,* Yiddish. Ivanov explains that he was an orphan raised in a non-Jewish town. Now he is introduced to the fact that he will need a permit to reside in the town and that even with a gold medal his place in the university is uncertain. To satisfy residence requirements he is taken to be registered as a dentist's assistant. The university will not be taken care of so easily. A quota based on merit has been replaced by a lottery. "They realized that within the past few years only the best fill the universities. . . . And pudding alone is not too good. . . . It might harm the stomach." Ivanov calls on his friend Shneyerson to help him through the initial difficulties and, of course, the Shapiros find that the gentile friend knows much more about what it is to be a Jew than the apparent Jew. The audience, privy to the change of identity, is treated to a series of jokes that turn on the confusion in the household. The "Gentile" has a Jewish *neshama* ("soul"), they say, even a Jewish nose. "You could change parts with your friend." It is clear that both young men are now attracted to Berta and, at her birthday party in the second act, when reasons for conversion are discussed, Shneyerson warns against it through his gentile mask. The family is perplexed further. When the two young men are alone, Shneyerson repeats his warning in blunt terms. Leave the Jewish daughter alone.

Ivanov will not relent. In the third act he visits Rabbi Levi Halperin and asks if he might convert to Judaism. The Rabbi discourages him. In the fourth act the family has gathered for the Passover seder with their gentile guest. Passover is the traditional season for the blood libel to arise. According to the anti-Semitic accusations, Jews use the blood of Christian infants in the making of *matzah*. We have already heard that a body has been found and such an accusation is brewing during the birthday scene, but the news is brought by the *shlimazl* Katz, and nobody takes what he says seriously. Now, in the middle of the seder, the police arrive looking for the Jew Shneyerson whose association with the hasidic family of Lubavich makes him a prime suspect. In these accusations rabbis and "saints" are said to have special need for the blood in their rituals. Ivanov is ready to go with the police, but the real Shneyerson jumps up, unmasks himself, tells the assembled company of the wager, and is arrested. Shapiro assures his family that nothing will happen to either of the young men. The whole story and the sudden revelation strike him as a wonder comparable to the deliverance from Egypt which they are celebrating. "Something like this happens once in ten thousand years! And only in the home of David Shapiro." The very perils associated with being Jewish are a further source of pride. The happy ending is confirmed by an epilogue in which we see everyone assembled at a railway station. Hershko and Berta are together. They are all saying goodbye to Ivanov. The Christian leaves and the Jews remain in this comic reversal of normal conditions in the diaspora.

If the play shows that "it's hard to be a Jew," it is harder to masquerade as a Jew and impossible to become one. The rabbi who discourages his conversion tells Ivanov that it is not enough to share the faith of the Jewish people. "These days all of us are a little weak in faith," he explains. "I am speaking of the *folk,* of peoplehood." For the rabbi the identity of the Jews as a folk is the result of the Exile. "One cannot become a Jew," he concludes. "To be a Jew one must undergo the whole Jewish diaspora."

Jewish identity as a result of the Jewish folk experience is perhaps the most continuous theme in Yiddish writing between 1881 and 1917. Jewish writers would also be alert to questions of class, but even as Sholom Aleichem satirizes the pretensions of the Jewish middle class he allows them to represent all Jews, scattered and dispersed. They too are the Jewish folk.

It is ironic that Sholom Aleichem's plays, written as a kind of living journalism, should have come into their own on stage one or two decades after their appropriate moment. By the time they were performed, they had ceased to be news. In Moscow they were performed as reminders of life in the old regime; in America they also spoke from the past. In both countries they achieved currency as an expression of a new effort to render Jewish folk material as art. Sholom Aleichem had succeeded in convincing his generation that the experience and the language of the Jewish folk could be made to serve the artist, the writer of stories, novels and plays. His success as an artist is his ability to have created the impression that he had left the language and the experience intact as a gift for generations of strangers.

CHAPTER 6

Toward the New

*N*IGHT, Elie Wiesel's novelistic account of his own experience in Hitler's camps, begins with a description of the end of a Jewish town in Hungary. The demise of the community is preceded by a change in the life of Moché the Beadle, a figure who is identified in a way that reminds us of his ancestry in Yiddish literature: "He was a past master in the art of making himself insignificant. Physically he was awkward as a clown. He made people smile, with his waiflike timidity." One day Moché is taken away with other foreign Jews living in the town. Nobody pays much attention. Several months later he returns and tells the people what has happened. The Jews were taken to the Polish border where they were given over to the Gestapo agents who forced them to dig their own graves. Moché has returned to tell the story of the massacre and to warn his former townsmen. They do not believe his story.

And as for Moché he wept. "Jews, listen to me. It's all I ask of you. I don't want money or pity. Only listen to me," he would cry between prayers at dusk and the evening prayers. . . . "They take me for a madman," he would whisper, and tears, like drops of wax, flowed from his eyes.[1]

The direction of the war is turning, the people say. Besides is it possible for Hitler to "exterminate a population scattered throughout so many countries? So many millions!" By the end of this short novel young Elie sees Jews chanting their own mourner's kaddish as they walk to their deaths certain that no generation of Jews will survive to pray for them.

The *shlimazl* had always been the bearer of bad news, but until 1943 it had been the privilege of the community not to believe him. "You think it's so easy to put one over on Kasrilevke?" the speaker asks in "On Account of a Hat." In "Dreyfus in Kasrilevke" Zeidel's townsmen beat him when he brings the news that the French captain has not been cleared of guilt. In *It's Hard to be a Jew* it is Katz, a little man perpetually smudged with ink to prove his right of residence as a printer, who first brings the news that another blood libel is brewing. Everyone calls him "Ketzele," little cat, and no one pays attention to him. Soon the police are at the door. Before Hitler, Sholom Aleichem understood the limits of Jewish comedy. When Fishl the Melamed recites the kaddish for his own soul in "Home for Passover" we are obliged to recognize the profundity of his own sense of doom however certain we may be of his survival.

After 1945 survivors like Elie Wiesel spoke to the world with authority that they were wise not to relinquish. *Night* is unabashedly autobiographical, but in it Wiesel does not pretend that his experience is unique. His story is embedded in what Yiddish literature had established as the typical Jewish life of the *shtetl* with its inevitable clown, Moché, transformed into a representative victim. Wiesel wrote *Night* in French, not Yiddish, and one result of the use of non-Jewish languages by modern eastern European Jewish writers is the establishment of the Yiddish paradigm of experience in world literature. Even before the enormity of Hitler's mass murder Sholom Aleichem established a literary relation to eastern European Jewry that would serve as a model for later writers including survivors of the Holocaust. He too saw himself as a survivor of a world that was fast vanishing. It was in New York, whose authenticity as a center of Jewish life he doubted, that Sholom Aleichem was finally compelled to write his own autobiography as a story of youth in an eastern European *shtetl*. The idea of a vanished world described with authority only by its survivors began as early as 1905 for the Yiddish writers.

By 1917 the major Yiddish writers of Sholom Aleichem's generation were all dead. They did not live to see the striking changes that would follow the passing of the czar. The boundaries of the Pale were removed, and with the disappearance of threatened sanctions from her Russian allies, England was free to offer the promise of a Jewish homeland in Palestine. The Balfour Declaration and the abolition of the Pale did not bring immediate improvement to Jewish life in Russia, but they signify the transformation of the world known to Sholom Aleichem, Mendele, and Peretz. Soon the most alert Yiddish critics were warning Jewish writers off the old material. Too many of the young writers continued to write "from memory about their small towns, and stayed with that, quickly draining themselves, repeating themselves, without any critical sense for what was new, for what was happening in Jewish life. The shtetl was our culture of yesterday. Whoever records it with naive infatuation, without understanding the revolution which took place within our Jewish society, is a man of the past."[2] The most vigorous of the young writers like Joseph Opatoshu remembered the rough edges of life in the old world and observed them in the new. New York low life in Opatoshu's stories registers a departure from the world of Sholom Aleichem comparable to Issac Babel's stories of Odessa. The very fact that Babel wrote in Russian indicates his distance from the Yiddish masters, but the Jewish theme that runs through the Red Army stories reveals his sense of his own role as a lonely mediator between two worlds. In one story he gathers in the body and the belongings of a rabbi's son into the car of a military train during the civil wars.

His things were strewn about pell-mell—mandates of the propagandist and notebooks of the Jewish poet, the portraits of Lenin and Maimonides lay side by side. . . . He died before we reached Rovno. He—that last of the Princes—died among his poetry, phylacteries, and coarse foot-wrappings. We buried him at some forgotten station. And I, who can scarce contain the tempests of my imagination within this age-old body of mine, I was there beside my brother when he breathed his last.[3]

Babel never outran the part of himself that died with the rabbi's son. In his translation of Sholom Aleichem's *Wandering Star* into Russian he retained the uneasy role of a mediator that brought with it doom in Stalin's time.

Revolution and Holocaust wrenched Babel and Wiesel out of the world described by the classical Yiddish writers, but the reality of eastern Europen life and literature is a living presence in their writing. For the literary imagination outright physical assault could not equal the sea change brought on by migration. In *World of Our Fathers* Irving Howe describes at length the fragmentation of *Yiddishkay* in America. American Jewish writers reflect the change:

Whatever these writers have gained from native American culture and the culture of international modernism—a great deal, of course—the Jewish side of their experience came to be fragmented. If, as J. V. Cunningham tells us, a literary tradition constitutes "a principle of order . . . which directs and determines the selection of the materials that enter into a work," then for the American Jewish writers the tradition of the Jews has figured more and more as lapsed rather than available possibilities. Knowing as much, the best of them have made this their central theme: the experience of loss as impetus to self-renewal.[4]

For many European Jews the dream of America offered the promise of Messianic fulfillment. For others it was never much more than an escape hatch, a refuge for failed speculators and ambitious moneymakers. This is the America that absorbs the culprits in Sholom Aleichem's stories and finally attracts Menakhem-Mendl. Most Jews who came to America expected that their lives would be made easier, but what they found at first were new difficulties. The move to America confirmed the urban tilt of modern times, and the cities of the new world proved no more prepared for the new masses than the cities of the old. Among the dislocated population of the American cities the Yiddish *folkshrayber* would find a willing audience. Surely the 100,000 people who walked past Sholom Aleichem's bier in 1916 were mourning the loss of a culture as well as a man.

The culture represented by Sholom Aleichem was, as we have seen, a culture of poverty. For the first generations of American Jews poverty was just a disappointment, not a cultural and a comical resource. One need only compare Michael Gold's *Jews Without Money* (1930) with Sholom Aleichem's adventures of *Mottel, The Cantor's Son* to see the difference. Mottel is made merry by need; the boy in Gold's novel is degraded and made bitter. For the immigrants America offered neither money nor complete cultural solace.

Republication of Gold's novel along with Henry Roth's *Call It Sleep*, the novels of Daniel Fuchs, and now the appearance of Howe's history have brought the immigrant experience to light. The Jewish writers who have flourished in America since World War II have generally left that experience in the shade though its disruptions probably account for the condition of alienation which these writers have come to represent. For the Yiddish writer in czarist Russia alienation was stamped into his passport. Whatever his disaffection, he shared this status with the entire Jewish community, and this condition was dignified by its kinship with a religious category, Exile. The Jewish writer in America has been cut loose from this spiritual and collective category though it is often convenient to superimpose the Yiddish example on what only seems to be a similar condition of modern alienation.

Occasionally in the postwar writing of American Jews we sense ourselves in company of characters transported directly from the milieu of Menakhem-Mendl. But in transit they become outlandish anomolies like the matchmaker in Bernard Malamud's "Magic Barrel." Shimon Susskind in "The Last Mohican" identifies himself as a classical *luftmensh:*

> "How do you live?" [Fidelman asks him.]
> "How do I live?" He chomped with his teeth. "I eat air."
> "Seriously?"
> "Seriously, on air. I also peddle," he confessed, "but to peddle you need a license, and that the Italians won't give me."[5]

He lives on air; he is harried by Gentile officials; he is, as he says, "always running," and he offers to speak Yiddish to his American counterpart, Fidelman, who prefers English. In his search for Susskind, whom he suspects of stealing his briefcase, Fidelman makes the rounds of the synagogues in the old Roman ghetto. As the title of the story suggests, Susskind is the last of his tribe, a strange survivor transported from the past by magic to haunt the American Jew. A common and, one may say, realistic character in Sholom Aleichem becomes a mystical interloper in Malamud's stories. Tommy Wilhelm in Saul Bellow's *Seize the Day* is also haunted by creatures who seem to derive from the Yehupetz of Menakhem-Mendl. They hang around a branch of the stock exchange on upper Broadway; they populate the cafes, hotels, and streets of the neighborhood; they hold out the promise of seductive speculation. And yet Wilhelm himself, with his self-made name, is detached from the element in which he moves. He has deleted his past as a mistake; he has sold out his future, and he is unable to grasp any more than a handful of Phenaphen and Unicap tablets in the present. "My son and I use different monickers," his father explains. "I uphold tradition. He's for the new."[6] But neither statement is true. In *Seize the Day* Bellow means to describe people who live without the support of tradition and without faith in what is new. The paraphernalia of Yiddish literature survives only as a reminder of what has been lost in its attenuation and migration.

More recently we have seen a new interest in the Yiddish sources of Jewish culture on the part of American writers. Though the movement coincides with new threats to Jewish survival in Israel, it expresses itself as a reassessment of the history and literature of eastern Europe. Lucy Dawidowicz edited *The Golden Tradition: Jewish Life and Thought in Eastern Europe* in 1967. Shortly after that Saul Bellow reexamined modern America as it manifests itself on upper Broadway, but this time through the consciousness of an old Polish Jew, Arthur Sammler. Sammler, the professorial journalist, is no *luftmensh,* but he speaks with the prophetic authority of someone who, like Wiesel's Moché, has climbed out of his own grave, a grave made for Jews.

It is unlikely that the Yiddish language will ever enjoy a revival, but the appearance of Uriel Weinreich's new Yiddish-English dictionary in 1968 opens the language to modern study. However Yiddish is approached it must not be read as a dead language. The stories of Issac Bashevis Singer are to be found in a Yiddish daily newspaper as well as in the *New Yorker.* Writers of Yiddish insist on the vitality of their language even after the diminution of their audience. In an untranslated story called "Der Zoken Hendler" ("The Stocking Seller") by the poet and novelist Chaim Grade, a former printer, actor, poet, revolutionary, and self-confessed failure speaks of his troubles to the author in a long monologue: "If a man cannot philosophize about his hard luck he must lose his sharp edge and dry up," he says. He goes on to explain a quarrel he has just had with his family: "You don't understand that if I were silent as that woman [a suicide] I too would have had to hang myself."[7] Silence is death. Speech is life. It is for this reason that Yiddish literature endures in the stories of its master, Sholom Aleichem, who captured language alive and preserved it as living speech.

Notes and References

Preface

1. Maurice Samuel, *The World of Sholom Aleichem* (New York: Alfred Knopf, 1943), p. 6.
2. Irving Howe and Eliezer Greenberg, eds., *A Treasury of Yiddish Stories* (New York: The Viking Press, 1954), p. 74.

Chapter One

1. Sholom Aleichem to M. Spektor in *Dos Sholom Aleichem-Bukh,* ed. Y. D. Berkowitz (New York: *Sholom Aleichem-Bukh* Komitet, 1926), p. 8.
2. Solomon M. Schwarz, *The Jews in the Soviet Union* (Syracuse: Syracuse University Press, 1957), p. 8
3. Simon Dubnow, *History of the Jews,* trans. M. Spiegel, (New York: Thomas Yoseloff, 1957), V, p. 8.
4. Marie Waife-Goldberg, *My Father, Sholom Aleichem* (New York: Simon and Schuster, 1968), pp. 66-67.
5. Sholom Aleichem, *Fun'm Yarid, Ale Verk fun Sholom Aleichem* (New York: Morgn-Frayhayt, 1937), XVI, 194. All citations of the Yiddish works of Sholom Aleichem will be made from this edition and will appear in these notes under the name of the specific work with volume number.
6. Sholom Aleichem, "Tit for Tat," *The Old Country,* trans. Julius and Frances Butwin (New York: Crown Publishers, 1946), p. 200.
7. Simon Dubnow, *History of the Jews in Russia and Poland,* trans. I Friedlander (Philadelphia: Jewish Publication Society of America, 1920), III, 10.
8. Ibid., II, 324-30.
9. Nokhem Shtif, "How I Became a Yiddish Linguist," in *The Golden Tradition: Jewish Life and Thought in Eastern Europe,* ed. Lucy S. Dawidowicz(Boston: Beacon Press, 1967), pp. 257-63.
10. For a thorough analysis of "Sholom Aleichem" as pseudonym see Dan Miron, *Sholom Aleykhem: Person, Persona, Presence* (New York: YIVO, 1972).
11. Gordon to Sholom Aleichem in *Dos Sholom Aleichem-Bukh,* p. 183.
12. "What our Literature Needs," trans. N. Halper in *Voices from the Yiddish,* eds. Irving Howe and Eliezer Greenberg (New York: Schocken Books, 1975), p. 26.

13. Dan Miron, *A Traveler Disguised: A Study in the Rise of Modern Yiddish Fiction in the Nineteenth Century* (New York: Schocken Books, 1973), p. 28.

14. The anecdote is told by Sholom Aleichem in "Auto-da-Fé," *Yidishe Shrayber,* XII, 29-40. Berkowitz analyses the relation of the two writers in *Dos Sholom Aleichem-Bukh,* p. 170.

15. In Yiddish the phrase "Me' darf sheyn geyn bagroben Yidn" is recorded in *Dos Sholom Aleichem-Bukh,* p. 169.

16. From a conversation with the Yiddish critic Baal Makhshoves quoted in *Dos Sholom Aleichem-Bukh,* p. 158. Sholom Aleichem describes his last meeting with Peretz in "A vok mit Y. L. Peretz," *Yidishe Shrayber,* XII, 69-78.

Chapter Two

1. "The Sins of My Youth," in *The Golden Tradition,* pp. 120-29.

2. "The Calf," trans. Jacob Sloan, in *A Treasury of Yiddish Stories,* pp. 97-111.

3. "The Penknife," in *Some Laughter, Some Tears,* trans. Curt Leviant (New York: G. P. Putnam's Sons, 1968), pp. 113-28.

4. "The Fiddle," in *The Old Country,* pp. 301-18.

5. *The Golden Tradition,* p. 125.

6. *Fun'm Yarid* is translated as *The Great Fair: Scenes from my Childhood,* trans. T. Kahana (New York: Collier Books, 1970). This episode appears on pp. 246-58.

7. "The Dead Town," trans. Irving Howe, in *A Treasury of Yiddish Stories,* pp. 205-13.

8. Mark Zborowski and Elizabeth Herzog, *Life is With People: The Culture of the Shtetl* (New York: Schocken Books, 1962), p. 299.

9. "Today's a Holiday—Weeping is Forbidden," in *The Adventures of Mottel, The Cantor's Son,* trans. T. Kahana (New York: Collier Books, 1961), pp. 9-21.

10. "Visiting with King Ahasuerus," in *Old Country Tales,* trans. Curt Leviant (New York: G. P. Putnam's Sons, 1966), pp. 51-64.

11. *The Great Fair,* pp. 17-18.

12. Ibid., p. 48.

13. "Gimpel the Fool," trans. Saul Bellow, in *A Treasury of Yiddish Stories,* pp. 401-14.

14. *Fun'm Yarid,* XV, 64. The English appears in *The Great Fair,* p. 246.

15. Ibid., p. 65. The English appears in *The Great Fair,* p. 246.

16. *Adventures of Mottel, the Cantor's Son,* p. 106.

17. Irving Howe, *The World of Our Fathers* (New York: Harcourt, Brace, Jovanovich, 1976), p. 574.

18. "Tsu di leyzer," *Ayznban-geshikhtes,* XXV, 7-8.
19. "The Bubble Bursts," in *Tevye's Daughters,* trans. Frances Butwin (New York: Crown Publishers, 1949), pp. 14-15.
20. *Menakhem-Mendl,* II, 157. His wife's response appears on p. 160 of the Yiddish edition, authors' translation.
21. "Dos Neye Kasrilevke," IV, 122. For the English see *Inside Kasrilevke,* trans. I. Goldstick (New York: Schocken Books, 1948), pp. 62-64.
22. "Sholom Aleichem," in *Yidishe Shrayber,* XII, 9-17.
23. *Yosele Solovey,* XXII, 79-83. This and other passages from *Yosele Solovey* have been translated by the authors.
24. Ibid, p. 115.
25. Ibid, pp. 260-61.

Chapter Three

1. *Yosele Solovey,* pp. 256-57.
2. *The Great Fair,* p. 3.
3. *Le Tailleur ensorcelé et autres contes,* trans. I. Pougatch and J. Gott-farstein (Paris: Editions Albin Michel, 1960), p. 7.
4. "The Station at Baranovitch," in *Old Country Tales,* pp. 193-205.
5. "The Town of the Little People," in *The Old Country,* p. 1.
6. "The Convoy," in *The Old Country,* p. 274.
7. "An Easy Fast," in *Tevye's Daughters,* pp. 172-79.
8. "If I Were Rothschild," in *Tevye's Daughters,* pp. 16-19.
9. "Three Little Heads," in *The Old Country,* pp. 329-35.
10. Quoted in P. Axelrod, "Socialist Jews Confront the Pogroms," in *The Golden Tradition,* p. 408.
11. "Home for Passover," in *The Old Country,* pp. 75-92.
12. "On Account of a Hat," trans. I. Rosenfeld, in *A Treasury of Yiddish Stories,* pp. 111-18.
13. This and a selection of "Tales of Chelm" appear in *A Treasury of Yiddish Stories,* pp. 620-27.
14. Y. L. Peretz, "Advice to the Estranged," trans S. Liptzin, in *Voices from the Yiddish,* pp. 19-21.
15. Y. L. Peretz, *My Memoirs,* trans. F. Goldberg (New York: The Citadel Press, 1964), pp. 69-70.
16. "Two Anti-Semites," in *Old Country Tales,* pp. 206-13.
17. Franz Kafka, *The Penal Colony,* trans. W. and E. Muir (New York: Schocken Books, 1961), p. 158.
18. "The Enchanted Tailor," in *The Old Country,* pp. 93-137.
19. Gershom Scholem, "Toward an Understanding of the Messianic Idea," in *The Messianic Idea in Judaism* (New York: Schocken Books, 1971), pp. 1-36.

20. The Tevye stories are collected in volume I of the Morgn-frayhayt edition. With the exception of "Tevye Wins a Fortune" (*The Old Country,* pp. 21-41; in Yiddish, "Dos Groyse Gevins"), the other stories are translated in *Tevye's Daughters.* They are "The Bubble Bursts" (pp. 1-15; in Yiddish, "A Boydem"), "Modern Children" (pp. 20-37; in Yiddish, "Heyntege Kinder"), "Hodel" (pp. 53-68), "Chava" (pp. 93-108), "Schprintze" (pp. 145-61), "Tevye Goes to Palestine" (pp. 203-24; in Yiddish, "Tevye fehrt keyn Eretz-Yisroel"), and "Get Thee Out" (pp. 257-72; in Yiddish, "Lekh-lekho").

21. Maurice Samuel, *In Praise of Yiddish* (New York: Cowles Book Company, Inc., 1971), p. 215.

22. *Life is With People,* p. 310.

23. "A Daughter's Grave," in *The Old Country,* pp. 402-11.

24. "Summer Romances," in *Stories and Satires,* trans. Curt Leviant (New York: Thomas Yoseloff, 1959), p. 79.

25. Sholem, *The Messianic Idea in Judaism,* p. 35.

Chapter Four

1. Walter Benjamin, "The Story Teller," in *Illuminations: Essays and Reflections,* edited with an introduction by Hannah Arendt, trans. H. Zohn (New York: Schocken Books, 1969), p. 87.

2. Roman Jakobson and Petr Bogatyrev, "On the Boundary Between Studies in Folklore and Literature," in *Readings in Russian Poetics: Formalist and Structuralist Views,* ed. L. Matejka and K. Pomorska (Cambridge, Mass.: The MIT Press, 1971), p. 91.

3. Mixail Baxtine, "Discourse Typology in Prose," in *Readings in Russian Poetics,* pp. 176-96. Victor Erlich, "A Note on the Monologue as a Literary Form: Sholom Aleichem's *Monologn*—A Test Case," in *For Max Weinreich on his Birthday: Studies in Jewish Languages, Literature, and Society* (The Hague: Mouton & Co., 1964), pp. 44-50. For the entire discussion of *skaz* the authors are indebted to Professor Ann Banfield of the University of California at Berkeley. See her "Narrative Style and the Grammar of Direct and Indirect Speech," *Foundations of Language* 10 (1973), 1-39.

4. Baxtine, *Readings in Russian Poetics,* p. 186.

5. Max Weinreich, "Yiddishkayt and Yiddish: On the Impact of Religion on Language in Ashkenazic Jewry," in *Mordecai M. Kaplan Jubilee Volume* (New York: Jewish Theological Seminary of America, 1953), p. 512.

6. Justin Kaplan in the introduction to *Great Short Stories of Mark Twain* (New York: Harper and Row, 1967), p. vii. "The Celebrated Jumping Frog" appears on pp. 79-95 of that edition. Ring Lardner's "Haircut" appears in *"Haircut" and Other Stories* (New York: Charles Scribner & Sons, 1954), pp. 9-21.

7. Jakobson and Bogatyrev, *Readings in Russian Poetics,* pp. 91-92.

8. "The Tenth Man," in *Some Laughter, Some Tears,* pp. 153-57.

9. "Sixty-six," in *Old Country Tales,* pp. 214-25.

10. "The Little Pot," in *Tevye's Daughters,* pp. 180-91. "A Bit of Advice," in *Some Laughter, Some Tears,* pp. 131-44.

11. *Life is With People,* p. 370.

12. "Some Like Them Cold," in *"Haircut" and Other Stories,* pp. 169-90.

13. *The Adventures of Menahem-Mendl,* trans. T. Kahana (New York: G. P. Putnam's Sons, 1969). Yiddish examples come from the Morgn-frayhayt edition, II.

14. Quoted in Dubnow, *History of the Jews,* V, 671.

15. "Dreyfus in Kasrilevke," in *The Old Country,* pp. 260-64.

Chapter Five

1. Boris Eixenbaum, "O. Henry and the Theory of the Short Story," in *Readings in Russian Poetics,* p. 231.

2. All quotations are the authors' translations from *Stempenyu,* XXI, 123-254.

3. From her introduction to *A Shtetl and Other Yiddish Novellas* (New York: Behrman House, Inc., 1973), p. 17.

4. *Yosele Solovey,* p. 126.

5. Ibid., p. 27.

6. *Stempenyu,* p. 198.

7. *Wandering Star,* trans. Frances Butwin (New York: Crown Publishers, 152), pp. 16-17.

8. Ibid., p. 28.

9. Ibid., pp. 51-52.

10. Ibid., p. 228.

11. Ibid., p. 234.

12. Ibid., p. 274.

13. Ibid., p. 201.

14. Ibid., p. 214.

15. Howe, *World of our Fathers,* p. 484.

16. A. Mukdoyni, "Sholom Aleichem as a Dramatic Writer," in *Sholom Aleichem Panorama,* ed M. Grafstein (London, Ontario: Jewish Observer, 1948), pp. 222-25.

17. *Tsuzeyt un tsushpreyt,* V, 41-97.

18. *In Shturm,* XXIV.

19. *Menshen,* V, 117-50.

20. *Dos Groyse Gevins,* V, 151-256.

21. *Shver tzu zeyn a yid,* XX, 9-164. An abbreviated version of the play which does not include Ivanov's visit to the rabbi appears in English trans-

lation as *It's Hard to be a Jew,* in *Sholom Aleichem Panorama,* pp. 236-66.

22. The Yiddish way of referring to the charge that Jews used Christian blood in certain rituals is the phrase "der blut bilbl" or libel. Of course this is the *Jewish* way of speaking of this event, not the Russian legal term. *Blood Libel* is the name given by Maurice Samuel to his book about Beilis.

Chapter Six

1. Elie Wiesel, *Night,* trans. Stella Rodway (New York: Hill and Wang, 1960), pp. 15-19.

2. Nokhem Shtif, "How I Became a Yiddish Linguist," in *The Golden Tradition,* pp. 261-62.

3. Issac Babel, "The Rabbi's Son," in *Collected Stories,* trans. W. Morison (New York: New American Library, 1960), pp. 191-93.

4. Howe, *World of our Fathers,* p. 587.

5. Bernard Malamud, "The Last Mohican," in *The Magic Barrel* (New York: Vintage Books, 1958), p. 164.

6. Saul Bellow, *Seize the Day* (New York: Fawcett World Library, 1968), p. 18.

7. Chaim Grade, "Der Zoken Hendler," in *Der Mames Shabosim* (New York: Cyco-Bikher Ferlag, 1959), p. 253.

Selected Bibliography

PRIMARY SOURCES

1. In Yiddish
Although a number of editions call themselves *Ale Verk fun Sholom Aleichem,* none is complete. For this study we have used a prewar edition that is uniform in text and pagination (though the volume numbers vary) with other printings undertaken after the author's death:
Ale Verk fun Sholom Aleichem. 28 volumes. New York: Morgn-Frayhayt, 1937.
This edition includes the primary works cited here with the exception of:
> *Blondzhende Stern (Wandering Stars).* New York: Jewish Press Publishing Company, 1922.
After the war part of the project to recover what was lost of eastern European Jewry included two notable attempts at the systematic collection of Sholom Aleichem's works. The first, begun in Moscow (Melukhe-Farlag "Der Emes," 1948), only achieved three volumes. This edition was to be arranged chronologically and therefore includes the earliest fiction as well as the novels written in the period of the *Folksbiblyotek (Sender Blank, Stempenyu, Yosele Solovey).* A more successful project was then initiated in Buenos Aires (Ikuf, 1952-). Thus far fifteen volumes of a projected thirty have appeared, including some of the major story cycles such as those of Tevye and Mottel.

A selection of personal material such as letters to and from the author can be found in:
> *Dos Sholom Aleichem-Bukh.* Edited by Y. D. Berkowitz. New York: *Sholom Aleichem-Bukh Komitet,* 1926.

2. In English
The Adventures of Menahem-Mendl. Translated by Tamara Kahana. New York: G. P. Putnam's Sons, 1969.
Adventures of Mottel, The Cantor's Son. Translated by Tamara Kahana. New York: Collier Books, 1961.
The Great Fair: Scenes from my Childhood. Translated by Tamara Kahana. New York: Collier Books, 1970.

Inside Kasrilevke. Translated by Isadore Goldstick. New York: Schocken Books, 1948.

The Old Country. Translated by Julius and Frances Butwin. New York: Crown Publishers, 1946.

Old Country Tales. Translated by Curt Leviant. New York: G. P. Putnam's Sons, 1966.

Some Laughter, Some Tears. Translated by Curt Leviant. New York: G. P. Putnam's Sons, 1968.

Stories and Satires. Translated by Curt Leviant. New York: Thomas Yoseloff, 1959.

Tevye's Daughters. Translated by Frances Butwin. New York: Crown Publishers, 1949.

Wandering Star. Translated by Frances Butwin. New York: Crown Publishers, 1952.

SECONDARY SOURCES

In this section we list what we consider the most important biographical, historical, linguistic, and critical work available in English. Even accepting the restriction to English, this must be regarded as a highly selective list. For a more extensive English and Yiddish bibliography see *The Field of Yiddish: Studies in Yiddish Language, Folklore, and Literature,* edited by Uriel Weinreich (New York: Columbia University Press, 1954).

1. Yiddish Life, Language and Literature

DAWIDOWICZ, LUCY S., ED. *The Golden Tradition: Jewish Life and Thought in Eastern Europe.* Boston: Beacon Press, 1967. An excellent introduction describes religious, national, and literary movements in various parts of eastern Europe. The text includes selections from memoirs of the best representatives of those movements.

DUBNOW, SIMON. *History of the Jews of Russia and Poland.* Translated by I. Friedlander. 3 volumes. Philadelphia: Jewish Publication Society of America, 1920. A history of the entire course of Jewish life in eastern Europe, it is of special interest when Dubnow enters the period of his own life which coincides with that of his friend Sholom Aleichem.

HOWE, IRVING AND ELIEZER GREENBERG, EDS. *A Treasury of Yiddish Stories.* New York: The Viking Press, 1954. The best brief critical introduction to the literature precedes a generous selection of stories by many authors.

———. *Voices from the Yiddish.* New York: Schocken Books, 1975. A selection of prose writing which includes Peretz' pronouncements on literature and nationalism as well as S. Niger's essay on "The Humor of Sholom Aleichem."

HOWE, IRVING. *The World of our Fathers: The Journey of the Eastern European Jews to America and the Life They Found and Made.* New York: Harcourt, Brace, Jovanovich, 1976. Reveals the full range of American Jewish life in its most populous center where Sholom Aleichem was to find a massive audience, a subject, and finally a home; includes an excellent account of the threatrical milieu of New York.

LIFSON, DAVID. *The Yiddish Theatre in America.* New York: Thomas Yoseloff, 1965. Useful appendices for names and dates of companies and productions.

LIPTZIN, SOL. *A History of Yiddish Literature.* Middle Village, N.Y.: Jonathan David Publishers, 1972.

SAMUEL, MAURICE. *In Praise of Yiddish.* New York: Cowles Book Company, Inc., 1971. Anatomizes various elements of Yiddish and gives a good sense of the language to those who may not speak it. Special references to Sholom Aleichem's use of Yiddish.

WEINREICH, MAX. "Yiddishkayt and Yiddish: On the Impact of Religion on Language in Ashkenazic Jewry." In *Mordecai M. Kaplan Jubilee Volume.* New York: Jewish Theological Seminary of America, 1943. pp. 481-514. An excellent study in sociolinguistics.

WISSE, RUTH. R., ED. *A Shtetl and Other Yiddish Novellas.* New York: Behrman House, Inc., 1973. A good introduction to a series of stories that removes sentimentalism from the description of *shtetl* life.

ZBOROWSKI, MARK AND ELIZABETH HERZOG. *Life is With People: The Culture of the Shtetl.* New York: Schocken Books, 1962. An intimate view of life from week to week in a slightly idealized *shtetl.*

2. Biography and Criticism

ERLICH, VICTOR. "A Note on the Monologue as a Literary Form: Sholom Aleichem's *Monologn*—A Test Case." In *For Max Weinreich on his Seventieth Birthday: Studies in Jewish Languages, Literature and Society.* The Hague: Mouton & Co., 1964. Places Sholom Aleichem in an important stylistic category.

GITTLEMAN, SOL. *Sholom Aleichem: A Non-Critical Introduction.* Mouton & Co., 1974. The subtitle is descriptive; a good companion to the stories.

GRAFSTEIN, MELECH, ED. *Sholom Aleichem Panorama.* London, Ontario: Jewish Observer, 1948. A collection of stories, plays, letters, memoirs and criticism; includes the Yiddish critics I. I. Trunk ("Menahem-Mendl of Kasrilevke") and A. Mukdoyni ("Sholom Aleichem as a Dramatic Writer").

MIRON, DAN. "Sholom Aleichem." In *Encyclopadeia Judaica.* 16
    volumes. New York: The Macmillan Company, 1972. The article
    divides the works into convenient categories; the encyclopedia is an
    excellent source for all material in Judaica.

————. *Sholom Aleykhem: Person, Persona, Presence.* New York: YIVO,
    1972. A study of the meaning of the pseudonym and the presence of
    the fictional author in the text of the stories.

————. *A Traveler Disguised: A Study in the Rise of Modern Yiddish Fic-
    tion in the Nineteenth Century.* New York: Schocken Books, 1973.
    On the nineteenth-century roots of modern Yiddish literature with
    special attention to Mendele and to the place of Sholom Aleichem's
    early writing in the making of a new status for Yiddish.

SAMUEL, MAURICE. *The World of Sholom Aleichem.* New York: Alfred
    Knopf, 1943. Invokes the recently lost world through an affectionate
    retelling of the stories.

WAIFE-GOLDBERG, MARIE. *My Father, Sholom Aleichem.* New York:
    Simon and Shuster, 1968. The only full-length biography in English;
    emphasis more on the familial than on the literary life of the author.

WISSE, RUTH R. *The Schlemiel as Modern Hero.* Chicago: University of
    Chicago Press, 1972. Traces the early sources and modern versions of
    a type amply identified in Sholom Aleichem.

Index

171